White Matter

Conversations about Racism and
How to Effect Meaningful Change

*Vanisha Parmar and
Aseia Rafique*

HERO, AN IMPRINT OF LEGEND TIMES GROUP LTD
51 Gower Street
London WC1E 6HJ
United Kingdom
www.hero-press.com

This edition first published by Hero in 2022

© Vanisha Parmar and Aseia Rafique, 2022

The right of the above authors to be identified as the authors of this work
has been asserted in accordance with the Copyright, Designs and Patents
Act 1988. British Library Cataloguing in Publication Data available.

Printed in Great Britain by CPI

ISBN: 978-1-91505-474-6

All rights reserved. No part of this publication may be reproduced, stored
in or introduced into a retrieval system, or transmitted, in any form or
by any means (electronic, mechanical, photocopying, recording or otherwise), without the prior written permission of the publisher. This book is
sold subject to the condition that it shall not be resold, lent, hired out or
otherwise circulated without the express prior consent of the publisher.

Contents

White Allies Matter

Preface

Vanisha Parmar

I am a diversity practitioner. This wasn't a role I happened to fall into or started because something else didn't work out. I made a conscious choice to go into this work because I wanted to address inequality and injustice and make a difference. The murder of Stephen Lawrence had a profound impact on me. At the age of fourteen I just couldn't get my head around why someone's life could be taken away for no other reason than the colour of their skin – what kind of world did we live in? I was deeply saddened, and as the incidents unravelled over the years before the killers finally faced justice this sadness turned into fury – how dare they? How dare they carry out such an horrific crime? What right did they have to take a son, a friend, a brother, just because he was Black? Even now, as I write this, almost thirty years later, I feel overcome with emotion – no matter how much I learn about race, racism and the reasons that it exists today not just in the UK but globally – this murder keeps it real for me. Racism is more than an academic discussion – its effects are far-reaching and fatal; we are talking about life and death, and this fuels my energy and passion. My work towards helping to create inclusive environments, to develop understanding and to address inequalities is my small contribution to making the world of work a better place. I hope, over the years, that I have helped people, organizations and – without sounding evangelical – in some small way, society.

Following the murder of Stephen Lawrence, my world view became very much focused through a racialized lens. I have been working in the diversity field for a number of years and I am conscious of how race plays out in everyday life. I have worked in a variety of organizations and over the years of meeting different people from all walks of life in the workplace, one thing that strikes me is how people interact in the world of work – particularly Black and Brown people. People of colour connect differently with one another compared to how they do with White people. I have noticed how some Black and Brown people, both at senior and junior levels, interacted with me and how they interact with White people, and this, coupled with my own experiences, started to shape some of my nuanced thoughts on racism, Whiteness and racial code-switching.

Human interaction and connection fascinate me, and I think the major factors that contribute to people enjoying a family gathering or a night out, or make the workplace an enjoyable place to be, in which people feel they belong, are authentic conversations and real connection. I personally appreciate those real conversations and feel that when these take place, people and organizations get the best experience. It is in those interactions, when people are themselves, have let their guards down and are able to share their authentic thoughts, that people feel safe. But in the workplace, I don't always see these happening. Of course, in that environment everyone needs to adopt a level of professionalism, and to some extent most don't ever really show their true selves. However, even when I take this into consideration, my observation is that there is an additional barrier that exists between some Black and Brown people and the rest of the workforce – the context is a racial one, not one of professionalism. The inability to be one's true self is detrimental to organizations and to the individual. These observations and the many informal conversations I have had over the years with Black and Brown colleagues and acquaintances led me to deepen my thinking on racial code-switching and navigating the workplace when you are Black and Brown. With the murder of George Floyd shining a brighter light on the lack of progress made on racial equity and equality in the UK, talking about these experiences is more important than ever. I feel honest conversations and action to dismantle the structures and systems of Whiteness that are pervasive play a key role in achieving genuine meritocracy. When this exists in all organizations, Black and Brown people will be able to progress towards and succeed in positions of power and influence, should they wish to do so, and be unapologetically themselves without fear of being judged. Yet, I find both the environment and culture in most organizations rarely allows the level of honesty that is required. My contributions to this book explore the reasons for the disparities that exist for Black and Brown people in the workplace are intended to provide an insight into how some Black and Brown people feel. I also hope to provide some understanding of what can be done to create an environment that is inclusive – beyond empty strategies and words – and why this is important.

I work with an enormous level of energy, commitment, positivity and passion, but this book comes from mixed emotions. It comes from frustration and fatigue on one hand, and hope and drive on the other. Frustration and fatigue because progress on achieving race equity is too slow; race inequality in the UK is not new and equity must occur at a much faster pace. Despite the volume of work organizations carry out on equality, diversity and inclusion such as events and initiatives, we are not there yet – why? I feel that the bar for measuring progress on race is often too low and focused on the wrong things. While there are some very good people and allies who are committed to creating the changes required to achieve equity, there are also others who quite enjoy the status quo. Hope and drive, because I see organizations and individuals wanting to do something; I see resources being put into the race equality agenda, and if these resources were to be directed into the right strategies, with good understanding and context of racism, change could be certain. I live in hope that we as a collective within society can make this happen. Drive because I want to live in a fair and just society, I have children – I don't want the colour of their skin and the negative assumptions and bias people hold to impact on their ability to achieve whatever they want. If I want this, then I feel I must work towards making it happen.

Aseia Rafique

Realizing I had to do more of the domestic work at home, and also manage my expectations for what I did outside of the home probably dawned on me when I consciously began to take note of the different expectations placed on boys and girls. Why did boys get to have more freedom? They were looked after better, told not to worry about cleaning up and, when unwell, were fretted over. Why were girls' and women's spaces and bodies constantly hijacked by those in authority, both men and women? I remember browsing a book on engineering, not really interested in the content but just flicking through, when I was told by my father to put the book away, because that was something I wasn't going to do. Such unfairness really bothered me, and has, I am sure, led me into the work I do today. Once I started to notice, I couldn't stop noticing. I began to see why things were difficult for those of us who not only come from under-represented backgrounds but less privileged backgrounds, and who are also consistently excluded, marginalized and micro-managed by others, in the home and in the workplace. In my workplace, it was almost impossible to bring attention to data showing the lack of Black and Brown people in senior management positions. Even when a change in policy highlighted that this would cause unequal access to certain roles, the senior leader responsible for initiating the change said the equality impact assessment was not to be shared. The usual process was to publish such equality impact assessments. This one I never saw again.

I remember reading about the 'NOTHING ABOUT US WITHOUT US' slogan used by the Disability Rights Movement, which stated that no policy should be decided by any representative without including members of the group(s) affected by that policy. I cannot believe how much we still need to use this slogan, and across all inequalities where they manifest themselves. I feel we need to remind ourselves to use any power we may have to support (and not deny) the opportunities and choices of others, whatever they might be. After all, if they are not a criminal or out to murder someone, why worry what others are doing?

Inequality damages us all. For me, the effect has been to try to show how individual behaviours are fed into a system that inevitably creates structural, systemic and deep-rooted bias. I have seen the views and opinions of others ignored because what they were asking for 'may take too long', was deemed 'too difficult to implement' or the current way of doing things was 'just the way it's done'. We have to keep chipping away at prejudice and bias. I hope we all continue to talk about – and work together to make – the changes we want to see.

We need our allies to show more honesty, activism and resistance to oppression. And we need to share more of our stories with one another.

Introduction

This book is for White allies interested in ways to reduce racism and discrimination in the workplace and to better understand where racist attitudes in society originate from. We talk about what racism looks like and discuss some of the complexity of the debate on racism. We also set out what White allies can do to support Black and Brown people by highlighting or challenging inequitable practices in the workplace, to being a voice of support for the Black and Brown people they know in their lives.

This book focuses on race and racism, and whilst some of our observations and points of view can be extended to other areas of diversity, we intentionally focus on race alone. That is not to say we don't accept and acknowledge intersectionality; this is really important and has an impact, but for us race is the central focus in these chapters, so as not to lose our train of thought or get distracted from what we want to say.

We met quite early on in our careers, while working in the same organization. As we left a meeting one day, we both looked at each other and rolled our eyes in annoyance and disbelief. Another meeting, we thought, where a room of senior (White) leaders discuss, at great length, racial inequality within the sector with no genuine commitment and intention of making change or holding people accountable, or discussion about the reasons why such disparities exist. Instead, we were met with hollow suggestions such as running a never-ending stream of workshops, events or training – meaningless engagement, in a bid to appease Black and Brown, to signal that work was underway, so the organization could appear busy on the diversity front! When a CEO chairs a race inclusion event and gives themselves a few minutes to 'prep' and read the notes that are handed to them, you know what you are working with – a lack of interest, priority and desire. This disappointment led us to want to work with organizations to provide real opportunity for change, drive direction and be honest by cutting through some of the bullshit we have observed. We want to see senior leaders, middle managers and allies authentically putting themselves forward and taking the time to invest in addressing racial inequality.

This book is for anyone who is interested in understanding some of the reasons why progress on race to date has been slow and is ready to take action to address racial inequality. We also want to engage those who hold the view that race plays no role in the world of work or has little impact on the lives Black and Brown people live. They feel that if Black and Brown people work hard, they will make it up the career ladder, breaking the glass ceilings, and we do on occasion see Black and Brown people in senior roles who worked hard to get there. However, the view that hard work is the single biggest component required for success is not the whole story. Many of the Black and Brown people have to work much harder than their White counterparts to reach senior positions. Some feel they have to tone down their 'Blackness' and 'Brownness' to fit in with the White normative values, for example, by toning down hairstyles and making a conscious effort not to appear 'too loud'. Furthermore, we hope this book not only validates what some Black and Brown people may be feeling, but also provides the impetus for positive and lasting change for organizations and individuals in the closed structures in which they find themselves.

Language is powerful and has the potential to help or hinder progress on race equity, and we recognize the fact that how people wish to identify themselves is a personal choice. However, we use the term 'Black and Brown' throughout our book as we feel this captures who we are speaking about more accurately than perhaps 'people of colour' – essentially we mean Black British, those from African, Caribbean and any other Black background, and British South Asian, those from an Indian, Pakistani and

Bangladeshi background. We do not use the terms Black and Brown to talk about people from an East Asian background and any references made to those from an East Asian background, we reference individually. We recognise that Black and Brown people are not homogeneous groups, and that each group faces some similar and distinct challenges, and within these categories there are a multitude of identities and nuances (religion, belief, history region, cultural and other).

Perhaps here we should explain the difference between equality and equity too, as we use both in the book and they are not interchangeable. Equality focuses on process – ensuring that everyone has been given the same fair opportunity, and equity is concerned with outcomes, recognizing that the same fair processes are not always successful and leave some people at a disadvantage due to a number of societal and organizational reasons.

Throughout the book we refer to senior leaders: these are board members, trustees, CEOs, directors, senior managers in the main, all of whom are integral in creating anti-racist practices. They are able to empower people to move beyond words to take actions that specifically address inequality. They are able to set the tone and insist on change to support inclusive workplace cultures that potentially lead to Black and Brown people being represented at all levels in organizations.

There are many books that discuss race and racism, so you might ask: how is this one any different? How did the book come about? Both of us are first-generation UK-born, and English is our first language (although we happily code-switch in the linguistic sense, to communicate and share anecdotes in languages of the South Asian diaspora which we belong to). The challenges that come with being a Black or Brown person and in particular, the surrounding nuances, are rarely brought to the forefront.

Our book is from the perspective of two South Asian Brown women born, educated and working in the diversity space as practitioners. It is brutally honest and comes from the years of experience of working closely with organizations and senior leaders, middle managers, HR professionals and other colleagues, but also from our conversations with other Black and Brown people. It includes our observations, understanding and thoughts on the reasons for the lack of progress to date and what can be done about it.

Both of us are discouraged by the overall pace of progress: it should not be difficult to bring equity and fairness into the workplace or in society but, as with everything, people – and especially those in positions of power – have got to desire that change. Clichés often arising from organizations are tedious: 'we are where we are', 'we've made great progress, but there is still more to do', 'we are aiming to achieve greater diversity... we are committed to diversity... we are passionate about diversity', and so on. The rhetoric is getting quite uninspiring, and we are loath to listen to it any longer. We suggest work that leads to material demonstrable actions, honesty and transparency rather than façade and pretence that is sometimes displayed. If one is inclined to make a difference, a genuine difference, then it is easier to step up and put this into practice.

But this is where it gets problematic, because, while many people, many senior leaders – mainly White people – often say the right things and use the right language, there are some who really don't want to step up, either because it's too much like hard work or they enjoy the privileges that come with their positions and Whiteness they experience. We have come across instances where, as diversity professionals, we are quizzed about 'why is so much being done on diversity and inclusion', when actually in practice, we feel there isn't enough of the right action being done.

Each chapter of the book offers suggestions and points for reflection that work towards challenging and addressing inequitable practices in the workplace and providing a voice of support for Black and Brown people. We know the majority of White people are not outright racist and our book is not about calling people out or pointing a finger – more about highlighting some of the difficulties that hinder progress and who can ease these difficulties. It seeks to move the focus from 'fixing' Black and Brown people to placing accountability and responsibility on senior leaders. For the two of us, writing these chapters and having these conversations have never been about 'them' and 'us', but more about calling out injustice and rallying for change – for the ultimate benefit of all.

We inherit the pain and trauma of migration, racist abuse and the violence our families experienced, as well as the subtler forms of racism that we are immersed in, and have witnessed the denigration of entire communities by politicians and the media. We are, however, less inclined than perhaps the generation before us to stay silent and accept such behavioural wrongs or blindly agree to well-trodden stereotypes and tropes, such as 'Black people are violent or lazy' or 'Muslims are terrorists'. As we've progressed from education to the workplace, we have begun to question and speak out about the simplified narratives that exist both in the place of work, and society. They have long presented to us bias, racism, inequality and prejudice.

The thoughts and observations we share in this book are not intended to be academic and scientific – this is intentional – rather, they are our perceptions based on our personal experiences and the formal and informal conversations we've engaged in over the many years with friends, colleagues, senior leaders and acquaintances whilst working in the diversity space.

The chapters in this book, although written in two distinct voices, interweave with each other reflecting on outlooks shaped by the places we have worked in and the cultures we have grown up in. We have so much to say and there just never seems to be a sufficient amount of time to say it in the meeting, at the event, in the training session, at the workshop – we knew it was time to put it down here, unapologetically. When we did start to speak we felt it resonated with so many other Black and Brown people. We started writing this book in 2020, at a time of vulnerability and openness, when talk about lived experience, racism, ethnicity and colour began to spill out more than it ever had, from the private into the public sphere and into everyday conversations. Black and Brown people had been speaking about these issues for years – it's just that those that needed to hear were not listening.

The murder of George Floyd and Black Lives Matter ripped up the rule book on speaking about racism for those that had never spoken about it so publicly before. Black and Brown people were demanding answers and there was a realization and acknowledgement (in some places anyway) of the lived reality of thousands of Black and Brown people from the UK (as well as from all over the world), of the current and historical impact of Whiteness. But we can change, and we can act. Now is not the time to remain silent but to be an active ally to friends, colleagues and family who experience discrimination. We know that as a White person, you have a level of power and influence, and speaking out is one way to reduce, revisit and revise injustice and inequality.

Vanisha and Aseia

1

THE SWITCHING GAME – OUR SECRET LIVES

Vanisha Parmar

When I look back at my life I have come to realize that I always did feel a little out of place, not necessarily in society but in institutions, be it school or work. Over the years, my experience, my interactions with others (both professionally and personally), life and global events urged me to reflect on what it means to be a person of colour, especially in the workplace. All the intricacies and nuances that come with being a person of colour are not openly discussed in the workplace in their entirety and while this is changing to a certain degree, to some extent the changes come with limitations. Rarely do we talk (in White spaces) about the full spectrum of racism: what it is, how it came into being and how it impacts and affects everyone. However, to manage expectations, I am by no means attempting to cover the entire spectrum of racism here; but there are some aspects of it I want to uncover, explore and discuss. As I grow in confidence, I have felt able to start speaking some of my truth. Although how Black and Brown people feel in the workplace and perhaps in their lives *should* be uncovered, to allow for the workplace to be a place where success in relation to career progression and feeling a sense of belonging are organizational norms for Black and Brown people, I feel that it is this truth many of us Black and Brown people bury, resulting in emotional and physical detriment to Black and Brown people and to society at large.

Context – growing up British-Indian

The majority of my early childhood was spent with others who were similar to me in terms of background. Of course, this is the case for many young people. My parents spent most of their free time with family and friends. Our weekends were filled with family visiting us (mainly because our grandparents lived with us). My grandparents had six children and between them there are fifteen grandchildren. There were many occasions where we were together as one big family. My childhood home brings memories of convivial ruckuses with food, drinks, Bollywood and laughter. Most outings and trips away were with members of the family (and Indian picnics of spiced potato sandwiches and other Gujarati savouries). When we were not with family, we visited extended family members or friends who had also migrated to the UK from Africa or India.

My grandparents were 'twice migrants' (a term that refers to people from South Asian origin who have migrated to the UK from countries outside South Asia). They were born in Gujarat, India, and came to England from Kenya, East Africa, with their children in 1964, as a result of policies that prioritized native Africans in the newly independent countries of Kenya, Tanzania and Uganda.[1] There were many who migrated to Birmingham, and it was these people and their children with whom I spent most of my formative years. From attending Gujarati language school two evenings a week to joining in religious and cultural celebrations and functions at community halls and temples almost weekly, my entire world was filled with people who shared a similar background and had a common view. In addition, my parents did not have a circle of diverse friends. They certainly had acquaintances from different backgrounds who they had met over the years, either through work or our neighbourhood – but they were not people that we interacted with socially. Not surprising with racial and immigration tensions high in the 1960s and 70s: my parents and grandparents came to the UK in the era of 'No Blacks, no Irish, no dogs'; and Enoch

Powell's notorious 'Rivers of Blood' speech.[2] This racism (along with other factors, I am sure) led to the establishment of a strong Indian-Gujarati community who shared common experiences of migration, economic status, educational level and a desire to create a sense of a strong Indian identity and unity, not to mention – a desire to survive.

School

I went to school in the 1980s, predominantly White, both in terms of pupils and teachers; I don't recall ever having a Black or Brown teacher and, some twenty-five or thirty years on, not much has changed. All ethnic groups, other than those from White British and White Irish backgrounds are under-represented in the teacher workforce.[3]

It was at school where I discovered I was 'different' and that this difference was not favourable. The racist and derogatory name-calling on our way home from school, something which Aseia experienced too and examines in detail in Chapter 2, was most certainly an additional reminder that we were different. I was able to brush off the name-calling and the not-so-polite requests to go back to where we came from, perhaps due to our strong family unit, sense of identity and support, but there was a sense of not being so welcome from a small minority of people. Ironically, Akala in his book *Natives: Race and Class in the Ruins of Empire* states that 'people in Britain were not informed that, over there, in the colonies, Caribbean and Asian people were being told that Britain was their mother country, and they were very much welcome by their loving motherland'.[4] Not quite the truth, and certainly not what my grandparents, parents and many like them experienced. Although it was at primary school where I experienced the most overt form of racism from children, it wasn't until secondary school that I started to feel that the ethnic and cultural differences between the majority-White group and me were much more pronounced.

The differences in the Indian culture and the White culture that surrounded me in my school days seeped into many aspects of my life. My evenings were filled with chores: helping my parents prepare traditional Gujarati dinners; helping to take care of my grandparents, with a huge focus on education and community. I also felt that my parents were much firmer in their parenting style. In contrast, my White friends, it seemed, had a different cultural experience and, to me, the differences were stark. It was common for my White friends to be allowed out to play until their curfew time, to be invited to each other's houses after school for 'tea' and sleepovers. I recall longing to be included, not least because the English 'teas' seemed more appetizing than the lentils and chapatti with pickle and papadums I would be having at home. While I was a little envious, I most certainly did not want any of my friends to visit me; I am sure if I had asked my parents, they would have been delighted. However, my grandmother spoke little English, she wore a saree and a bhindi; she burned incense around the home and said her prayers loudly while ringing a bell. Our house had Indian art and religious artefacts on the walls and around the home, and there was always a strong aroma of Indian cooking. I was embarrassed and feared being seen as different. The irony: these things are now perhaps essential for the journey of spirituality and 'wokeness' that many in the West seek and take part in.

How does this cultural difference impact Black and Brown people? According to Beverly Daniel Tatum, in the Book *Why Are All the Black Kids Sitting Together in the Cafeteria?*,[5] this growing [racial] awareness can be triggered by the cumulative effect of seemingly minor incidents that young people experience. The perception I had of myself was one of difference and she suggests 'these perceptions are shaped by the messages that we receive from those around us'[6] and as we enter adolescence the racial content of those messages intensifies.[7] This is a significant point as this impact can go on to shape us in adulthood, and very much so in my case.

In stark contrast to school, from about the age of sixteen onwards during college, my social circle was made up almost exclusively of Black or Brown people. It seemed almost most of us naturally gravitated towards one another, which in turn created a sub-community in the college canteen. And, like most college, university canteens and communal places, there was a visible and profound segregation. This is not uncommon human behaviour and in social science is referred to as homophily: a natural tendency to associate with others with similar traits.[8] I did have White friends – good friends – but our friendships eroded rapidly during college. The college was in an affluent and middle-class area of the West Midlands and predominantly White – although, until a few years ago, I didn't give too much thought to how White it was; perhaps because it was on the periphery in the sense that I was not directly engaging with it.

Tatum suggests that self-segregation is a form of coping and a much-needed mechanism for support. I agree; it is somewhat natural to want to surround ourselves with people with whom we have much in common, particularly when we are not from the dominant or majority group. Tatum states that the 'developmental need to explore the meaning of one's identity with others who are engaged in a similar process manifests itself informally'.[9] This congregation in the canteen most certainly was informal and in no way made me feel like I was a 'minority' during college. The group of people with whom I had proactively surrounded myself understood my background, the values I grew up with, my culture, the family nuances and dynamics – even my incense-burning, bell-ringing and saree-wearing grandmother. In fact, they understood probably nearly every aspect of my life. It wasn't anything explicitly discussed, but an undercurrent of understanding existed, and this played a significant role in building identity and confidence. To be anything other than myself, to 'fit in', didn't once cross my mind once. Almost immediately, the sense of 'other' I had felt previously evaporated.

My university experience was similar; I moved away from my parents' home and this sub-community was created once again and led to an even further exploration of my British-Indian heritage. I joined the University's Asian and Hindu Society and this identity I was enjoying was all-consuming and a safe space. It was a world in which I was very comfortable, with my peers' interests and background all similar to mine. My identity, with all its facets, were understood as the norm by those around me. I was proud and confident of my British-Indian heritage and I, like many, was living in a swirl of two cultures. Neither explicitly made me feel like I didn't belong. I felt like I had the best of both worlds and I was quite privileged. Looking back now, I see the incongruity and recognize how oblivious and naive I was – I deemed it necessary to congregate in these safe spaces for protection or perhaps survival in a world where subconsciously, I did not quite fit.

Navigating Whiteness

Whiteness – a term to capture all of the dynamics that go into being defined and/or perceived as white and that create and reinforce white people as inherently superior through society's norms, traditions and institutions. Whiteness grants material and psychological advantages (white privilege) that are often invisible and taken for granted by whites.[10]

My first job immediately after graduating was in the higher education sector, which was a largely White middle-class sector, similar to secondary education sector, and still remains so some twenty years on.[11] I was no longer within a circle of similar people. In fact, I was a minority in the workplace; of course, I was always a minority, but now I *felt* like a minority – it wasn't that I felt completely excluded, but the differences were visible. The world of work was new terrain and I sensed immediately just how White *it* was and just how 'White' I wasn't. These thoughts did not wholly consume me, but in the back of my mind they burned like a small flame. The feelings were sharpened not by what anyone had ever said to me directly, but rather, it was the subtle incidents and realizations that I use as points of reference. Everything seemed so *White*, meaning there was a lack of diversity that I had experienced at school and college: conversations about music, weekend activities, books, places of interest, food and so on. It most certainly felt different.

Sociologist Pierre Bourdieu[12] in his work on class and habitus claims that 'those who don't experience immediate adaptation to the situation, feel conscious, acutely reflexive and ill at ease.'[13] On reflection, this very much resonates with me. Like many other people of colour, I bury this feeling, not giving it energy, and try to just get on. Some don't recognize the racial element – ever. I was young, in my twenties, trying to navigate a majority White space in absence of my usual comfort blanket, the 'sub-community' made up of other Black and Brown people. I knew this world was very different to what I was used to and somewhere deep-rooted was the understanding that I was expected to 'fit in' and assimilate to the majority culture, at work at least. Why? Where did this come from? Layla F Saad[14] suggests that conditioning to believe in White superiority happens from childhood through how history has been taught; how race is spoken about; how we have educated and taught White superiority through curricula that lean towards a White-based narrative; the media representations of White people and people of colour; and in the world of work it is likely that White superiority is upheld 'through a lack of representation of BIPOC (Black, Indigenous, and People of Colour) at leadership levels, through inclusion and diversity policies that are about optical allyship and through HR policies (implicit and explicit) that tone police[15] and marginalize employees who are BIPOC'.[16] The more I move up in my career and work with senior colleagues, the Whiter and more middle class it becomes. The differences are obvious – to most Black and Brown people, anyway. Black and

Brown people notice the lack of ethnic diversity immediately in a meeting, on a panel, talking about racism; whatever it is, we notice Tatum suggests: 'People of colour are isolated and often in the extreme, opportunities to connect with peers of colour are few and far between.'[17] This, I am sure, brings with it the feeling of exclusion or alienation.

Code-switching

I never really had a term for it before; a term for the pressure to conform to a standard of Whiteness, trying to fit into and navigate White spaces. In fact, I was oblivious to it in my younger years. In addition, I have never spoken about it publicly before either, yet it has been at the back of my mind. There had always been an under-current that murmured softly within me and of late the thoughts have solidified. Following the resurgence of the Black Lives Matter movement there is a sharper focus on race and ethnicity. There seems to be some space to express, discuss and reveal. I think the conversations around racism and race are different to what they were in the past, and while not much progress on racial equity has taken place when we consider data and information, conversations *have* progressed; and most certainly different to when I embarked on my professional career some twenty years ago.

This veneer that I presented – not with the aim of trying to put a different version of myself forward, but to appear as if I had earned my place at the (White) table – was, as I have now come to learn, code-switching. Traditionally, code-switching is the practice of switching between languages in different situations and contexts. In 1977, Carol Myers-Scotton and William Ury recognized code-switching as the 'use of two or more linguistic varieties in the same conversation or interaction.'[18] With this definition in mind, I most certainly engaged in the act of code-switching when I was conversing with my grandparents in Gujarati and I'm sure most multi-lingual people do too. It is common to pepper conversations with words from another language when you're bilingual. However, moving away from traditional linguistic definition to a wider one we can see how racism plays its part. To some, code-switching can mean a more 'professional' way of speaking. In relation to people of colour it could manifest as switching between speaking Patois in the home and with friends to 'standard English' at work or sharpening dialect to sound 'White' or 'Whiter'. However, for me, the definition goes much further than that. World-renowned scholar W E B Dubois in his book *The Souls of Black Folk* (first published in 1903) talks about double consciousness[19] and the experience of Black people in America post-slavery. He describes this double consciousness as a 'sense of always looking at oneself through the eyes of others, of measuring one's soul by the tape of a world that looks on in amused contempt and pity.'[20] This wider understanding and definition I feel, captures the principle that runs through the act of racial code-switching: seeing one's self through the eyes of others. The 'others' in this case are the systems of Whiteness. When I speak of code-switching, I am speaking of an all-encompassing act. I am speaking of the alteration of Black and Brown people's tone, dialect, language, dress code, what is spoken about what isn't spoken about, what we eat, what we watch and listen to, how loudly we listen to it – in fact, potentially every essence of our being in an attempt to fit in in the workplace and not to be seen as deviating from the (White) 'norm'. But these are not necessarily conscious acts – they are learned and second nature, so much so that in some of my conversations with Black and Brown people, it was apparent that they had not given it much thought, if any at all – it was our conversation that allowed them to connect the dots.

Subconsciously, I had learned to switch in professional White spaces – I wanted to fit in seamlessly and to create the perception that I belonged. I found myself speaking differently; I altered my accent and made my slight Asian dialect undetectable, in a bid to not only sound Whiter but to appear Whiter too. Why did I do this? Was it lack of confidence, being young, lacking experience?

It could be argued that it was all of those things. However, Kwame Ture et al[21] suggest that there is a feeling that the closer you are to White, the better you are. Tatum suggests that those who are in regular contact with White people adopt an understanding that 'their ability to make it depends in large part on their ability to conform to those values and behaviours that have been legitimized by White culture.'[22] In order to 'make it', she argues, some will adopt a raceless persona to gain approval. This raceless persona was the one I was trying to put forward to some extent, but only ever in the realms of work, and more so when I was younger. This raceless persona can be problematic within the communities of Black and Brown people and, although I have not experienced it, I recognize the derogatory remarks and contempt for those who are perceived to embody Whiteness. The requirement to code-switch, for me, occurred most significantly in relation to talking about, and challenging racism, particularly in my younger years. I was mindful of White people's feelings; not wanting to hurt or make anyone feel uncomfortable. There have been many occasions where I didn't speak up, didn't call it out, didn't challenge to avoid 'that awkward moment', and for fear of being perceived as a troublemaker, or as an outsider who was not to be trusted because I didn't think like the majority group. I code-switched to portray a version of me that would be accepted. Resmaa Menakem, in the book *My Grandmother's Hands: Racialized Trauma and the Mending of Our Bodies and Hearts*[23] talks about the feelings that some people of colour hold in a bid to protect White people. He explains that while 'White bodies' (White people) and 'Black bodies' (Black people) shift into self-protection mode when they experience each other there is a difference with Black bodies. 'The Black body is habituated to shift into soothing the White body as a self-protective strategy.'[24] This is similar to the ideas suggested by Robin DiAngelo in *White Fragility*.

I want to be clear: when I speak of Whiteness, I am not referring to individuals and individual acts, but rather, to a system that works in favour of and to the benefit of White people due to the way in which it is set up. The standards and boundaries that are set and established benefit the White majority. It is a system that perpetuates a culture where Whiteness is deemed to be superior. The ideologies, social norms and behaviours associated with White culture are the comparative standard to which all races are objectified.[25] Once we can understand this, it is easier to comprehend not just my experience, but also other people's experiences. This standard is set and all of us, whether we know it or not, are trying to attain this standard.

I am sure there are many that will try to explain my experience through the lens of social mobility (I come from working-class roots) and/or age or some other factors. I recognize that these intersect with each other; however, my class background wasn't the issue for me – the issue was the sheer Whiteness of the world I was in. Certainly, with age we tend to gain more confidence in our identities and who we are, racialized or not. We have more world experience, insight and wisdom. The fact remains, however, that these places of work: institutes, offices, boardrooms and committees are all White in every aspect. And the desire, unwittingly perhaps, to fit in is ever so prevalent because I, and many others, feel our success depends on it.

I recall the Black comedian Curtis Walker from *The Real McCoy* (a BBC comedy sketch show which featured a host of Asian and Black comedians)[26] who I saw perform on stage in the late 90s. In one segment of his show, he talked about leaving his house for work and explains his journey starts with playing dancehall[27] loudly in his car, with the windows wound down. However, as he gets nearer to his place of work, the 'Whiter' what he is listening to becomes, and by the time he has arrived he is tuned into Classic FM. I remember the laughter that accompanied this anecdote. However, the message it conveyed was far from funny: wanting to portray a different version of yourself in a racialized context comes with some pain and trauma that most internalize, bury or laugh off. This occurs in an attempt to 'just get on with it' or to come to terms with a reality of which Black and Brown people have little agency in some situations. Code-switching most often takes place in environments where negative stereotypes don't align with what is considered normative or appropriate for that environment, most commonly in academia and in places of employment.[28]

This is interesting to me, not least because most large organizations invest in diversity, inclusion and equality, and powerful statements such as the one below are not unusual; and a simple internet search can bring up many similar examples:

Bringing different people, with different ways of thinking, together in collaboration is how positive change happens; it's essential to our success. We're determined to create a truly inclusive firm that fully reflects the make-up of our society. A place where every individual feels they can be their real selves, be heard, and respected. Where all can thrive, develop and succeed based on talent, regardless of ethnicity, gender, sexual orientation, or any other dimension that can be used to differentiate people from one another.[29]

Despite the words we see above, and the words that are spoken, in organizations, most Black and Brown people are compelled to alter themselves in some way. What was it that made me feel being myself was not good enough and that I should try to become more like the majority/dominant group? There is never an explicit request or requirement to do so. It is never discussed (openly); yet 'Whiteness' is entrenched as being the ultimate standard to be achieved and the socialization into accepting the Whiteness as the norm. And while Black and Brown people, as a result of this may feel inferior, there may be many White people who have a deep sense of superiority and act on this belief in the practice of their lives[30] which validates this ideology. Studies show when identities are not consistent with the requirements of the workplace people of colour find it hard to express their true selves; however, the existence of a supportive environment creates a feeling of psychological safety. Research shows that for White people a positive diverse environment and psychological safety are less important.[31]

As I mentioned earlier, I recognized from a young age that I was different, and I did feel a sense of being 'othered'. Interestingly, research suggests that White children develop the sense of superiority as early as pre-school.[32] The societal messages delivered daily through television programmes, books and all other media platforms in turn reinforce this idea. In *White Privilege: The Myth of a Post-Racial Society* the author Kalwant Bhopal states that 'Whiteness is based on an identity that is considered superior to all other identities.'[33] Bhopal claims that White people are at the top of the hierarchy by virtue of their White identity – this results in them holding power over people of colour (either consciously or unconsciously). The invisible, yet powerful tool of Whiteness is rarely spoken about in the mainstream and even less so in organizations at a mainstream level, yet the impact of it is huge and leads to this panoptic type of code-switching.

Because it is rarely spoken about, even amongst Black and Brown people, I wanted to explore and discuss code-switching with others to gain insight. I have never spoken about code-switching and I wanted to know if others' experiences were similar to mine. To help shape my thoughts I spoke to friends, acquaintances, those in my professional network and family members, mostly senior professionals who identified as Black, Brown or White. I am eternally grateful for their honesty and openness. Particularly, like me, most had not discussed this subject previously and I acknowledge sharing personal thoughts and experiences comes with some level of emotional levy and vulnerability.

My conversations are not intended to be academic research but rather, an insight into how some Black and Brown people navigate Whiteness. My conversations certainly triggered memories and reflective thoughts for most of the people I spoke to. At the beginning of our conversations, a few stated they hadn't code-switched; however, as we got into into the conversation and as they reflected, they realized that they had. Being afforded the space to reflect allowed them to recognize that there were times when they had altered themselves to appear closer to White – something that Menakem[34] proposes is important for healing and responding to racism. Although many were not familiar with the term, my experience resonated with them and some had a strong sense of recognizing themselves from a racialized lens that stemmed from a young age. Interestingly, there were a few people I spoke to who grew up within an environment that wasn't so strong in their cultural identity; these people didn't feel the pressure or the need to code-switch so much because they felt close to 'White' and were quite comfortable in White spaces – they are also fairly successful in their professions. And although they didn't view themselves as different, particularly growing up, they were very aware as they moved up to senior positions in their careers that the world *did* view them so. One of those women, after we talked for a while, realized that perhaps her parents had code-switched to better fit into the system of Whiteness to ensure professional success; so, as she put it, 'to make their children's lives easier.'

I have outlined some of my conversations on race, identity and code-switching in more detail at the end of this book (see page 166).

Below are some of the anecdotes from my conversations about code-switching in particular:

- *I am never myself; I am always on edge, but it does depend on context. I am less concerned in public, however in employment, I completely change; I change in the office.*

- *I am very aware of how I am perceived; I change quite a lot about me. My diction, my posture, my body language – this is down to the colour of my skin.*

- *I don't react to frustration in a natural way; I don't want to be a stereotype.*

- *I 100 per cent code-switch; I don't trust the diversity narrative and I don't think I can be myself. Being myself will result in a detrimental impact. I know it will.*

- *I am always conscious that I will be taken in the wrong way and I rarely speak about racism [or] identity politics.*

- *I am extra nice to make White people feel relaxed and comfortable and think I am OK, so I can fit in.*

- *You have to 'play the game'. You have to code-switch or you just wouldn't be successful.*

- *In new spaces, I am very nervous about the impression people may get of me, so I am uber-friendly and smiley.*

- *I don't want to talk about race or racism; so I change how I talk and appear to be neutral because it feels like my real thoughts won't be accepted and I will be looked upon negatively.*

- *Of course, [I code-switch]; if we didn't, we wouldn't make it in the professional sphere.*

- *I didn't realize I did, but I guess I do – I have anglicized how my name is pronounced for sure.*

- *I don't always code-switch. I am fairly comfortable in White spaces and I think I am quite like a White person myself.*

The general consensus amongst the Black and Brown people I spoke to was that White people, because of the privilege Whiteness affords them, were oblivious to the act of racial code-switching – how would they know? Feminist and anti-racism activist Peggy McIntosh, in her paper 'White Privilege: Unpacking the Invisible Knapsack', talks about unearned privileges she is afforded because of her Whiteness, stating, 'White privilege is like an invisible weightless knapsack of special provisions, maps, passports, code-books, visas, clothes, tools and blank checks.'[35] She goes on to say, 'My skin colour was an asset for any move I was educated to want to make. I could think of myself as belonging in major ways, and of making social systems work for me. I could freely disparage, fear, neglect, or be oblivious to anything outside of the dominant cultural forms. Being of the main culture, I could also criticize it fairly freely.'[36] The sad fact is that a racism for Black and Brown people that leads to hiding parts of ourselves and adjusting to fit in is just part and parcel of professional and corporate life; that's assuming you want to climb the career ladder. And although the same can be said for those who identify as LGBTQ+ I think this is different because you are not able to conceal the colour of your skin as you could your sexuality perhaps. White people just don't have the same sense of levelling up to the invisible, but ever-so-present standard of Whiteness because, of course, they are White. When I have shared these anecdotes with White friends they have been stunned. From some of my conversations there was a suggestion that code-switching wasn't racialized; we all code-switch to some extent, right? Yes, of course we do: in interviews, in new job roles, meeting new people. This is true however; code-switching for White people, when they are the majority is not racialized – its momentary, circumstantial because of the privilege that is afforded. My conversations also brought to light how naturally and subconsciously Black and Brown people code-switched. I also found when White people who had positive experiences with a diverse range of people, for example had good friends from diverse backgrounds, they were more likely to view Black and Brown people more positively in the work place. In addition, they were aware of and understood racism and the challenges much better.

Key highlights from my conversations:

Ultimately, people of colour code-switch because they want to increase their opportunities of being promoted and of being able to survive the world of professional and corporate organizations and environments.

People did not want to be associated with their 'Blackness', cultural background or ethnicity too much for fear of not getting on in their careers.

There was a challenge in getting the balance right in bringing enough of oneself to work to feed into the diversity narrative in a way that was comfortable and easy for White people. Too much could jeopardize the chances of success.

Black people did not want to be othered and play into the racialized stereotypes, such as being seen as a threat or as aggressive.

There was a desire to want to fit in with those with power and influence and to be seen as similar, for fear of not making it because you are deviant from the [White] norm.

There was a recognition that when one didn't engage in code-switching it most certainly had a detrimental impact on career, in some cases taking longer to reach the desired career goals.

Racial code-switching came with a level of emotional tax.

Those who grew up in a majority White environment with predominantly White friends into adulthood didn't feel the need to code-switch so much and were most comfortable in White spaces; however, they still recognized and/or experienced racism in some form or another.

What impact does code-switching have?

Most of the people with whom I spoke felt that code-switching did come with some adverse impact and recognized it was deep-rooted and entrenched into daily life. Some talked about the emotional tax that came with it and how draining it is to code-switch. McIntosh recognizes the impact in her paper and states: 'In proportion as my racial group was being made confident, comfortable, and oblivious, other groups were likely being made unconfident, uncomfortable, and alienated.'[37] In my conversation with Dr Tina Mistry, founder of the Brown Psychologist,[38] she shares her views on the impact of code-switching.

Dr Tina Mistry, Psychologist and founder of the Brown Psychologist

What are the effects of code-switching?
There are parts of us that exist that sometimes we choose not to expose and if we feel that we don't fit in, or we are told we don't, our natural response is to shut down. However, shutting a part of yourself has an impact; we all need to be seen and heard. If this continuously takes place in the workplace it leads to attachment difficulties and feelings of shame, turmoil and inner conflict.

We can experience impostor syndrome and our insecurities become profound. You become uncertain of yourself and I have seen in my practice that clients start to doubt their abilities – the result of which is frustration, anxiety and anger; or in some cases, depression.

The White majority seems to be the accepted comparator. This is also the case for class too – whose class are the class divisions made up from? This is rooted in Whiteness and it's complex.

How do we move forward?
There must be an acknowledgement of the existence of the system of oppression and an understanding that when Black and Asian people are given the (subliminal) messages that

we're not enough – this leads to racial trauma. Racial trauma is a cognitive and physical experience.

The oppressor sees a Black person as a threat to the system; this energy is picked up on by Black and Asian people. It is a bi-directional and multifaceted experience. However, for many White people they don't even know they're doing it. White people are not in tune to this energy and are most certainly not aware that this energy interaction is even taking place.

It is well documented that those who are able to be themselves at work are most likely to thrive, and psychological safety at work is essential to diversity. The mental health impact of racial code-switching on those who practise it cannot be played down.

Menakem[39] suggests that navigating Whiteness and White supremacy can bring racialized trauma to our bodies, but this trauma is not limited to just Black bodies. It extends to White bodies too in the way that White bodies feel they should respond and behave towards Black bodies in relation to the necessity to maintain power dynamics to survive.

How do we address code-switching?

There is no quick win: to not engage in code-switching means to unlearn so much, to take on a system of Whiteness and to be vulnerable; this is a risk many are not willing to take. Besides, for a truly anti-racist approach, that is, one that accepts that the current processes make it harder for people of colour to thrive and flourish, organizations must make the necessary changes, not just individuals. Organizations must start to address this culture of Whiteness that is so deeply entrenched. We must remember, racial code-switching takes place due to the concerns people of colour have over the (perceived or actual) negative professional consequences of aligning with their true cultural and authentic Black or Brown selves. Therefore, building trust and understanding in any work environment is essential to progress. The leadership and culture of an organization is a key asset to addressing code-switching, and where I believe it starts. The culture sets the tone of an organization and will determine how authentic people are able to be. If the desire is to be accountable for change, to create a truly inclusive organization, one that values and respects individuality, diversity and racial equity,[40] then change is possible. Senior leaders and middle managers have the power and influence to make decisions, authorize action and lead by example to support change and push the boundaries of the norm. If organizations get this right, everything else falls into place much easier. Changing policies and culture to achieve racial equity benefits everyone.

I outline some points to consider for your organization:

REFLECTIONS TO SUPPORT GOOD PRACTICE AND WHAT TO AVOID

Education and awareness

- Have you educated your senior leaders and senior decision-makers such as Boards, senior management teams and middle managers on the structures that exist and create barriers for Black and Brown people, this can include Whiteness and privilege, it is going to be difficult to make progress without context and understanding.
- Do you understand that diversity at all levels, and at decision-making tables lessens the need for racial code-switching?
- Are you aware and mindful of how your world view is created? For example, are the main characters in mainstream media often White? What effect might that have on shaping your perceptions? Think about what you watch, listen to and read, as well as the places you visit

34

- do they provide a parochial world view?
- Consider stereotyping and bias and the impact these have. Check yourself – what are *your* thoughts based on?
- Do you take time to understand the people of colour in your organization?
- Be open to learning and ask about Black and Brown people's experiences of life and work and take an empathetic view to understand how others may experience inequality.
- Remember, if people don't tell you how they are feeling (because that in itself is draining and can make most Black and Brown feel quite vulnerable) you can safely assume most people code-switch at some time. Most institutions are built on a system of Whiteness, so there is always work to do.
- Take action on anything you learn about how people are feeling. It shows commitment when learning is turned into tangible action to promote change.
- Don't single people out and request they tell you how they are feeling in the work environment. This can put people on the spot and make them most uncomfortable. However, you can provide opportunities for people to share how they feel, should they wish to – for example, with staff attitude surveys and safe-space networks for people of colour.

Creating inclusive environments

- Do you have a plan of ongoing work? Remember that a truly inclusive organization requires constant work – rather than one-off actions.
- Do the words in your vision, values and strategic plans transfer into direct, innovative action? This is a good (but not the only) place to start. When people see that real

action is taking place to promote a culture of inclusion and diversity at the decision-making tables and rooms it creates trust.

- Senior leaders – are you using your power and influence to demand diversity at senior levels and promote a culture that welcomes diversity of people and views? When senior leaders make this a priority and reward good practice, this sets the tone and others in the organization will usually follow suite.
- Senior leaders – are you challenging the culture that perpetuates Whiteness as the ultimate standard and equipping teams to carry out work to address this operationally?
- Are you creating a culture that invites diversity and difference to the table of decision-making to avoid groupthink? This is not about diverse individuals filling seats or the 'token' person of colour who quite possibly code-switched to get into that senior position, but rather about people who are committed to promoting equitable outcomes, diversity and inclusion in addition to bringing new perspectives, ideas and ways of working.
- Is there space for Black and Brown people to come together if they wish and do you check in with this space periodically through formal management structures with the aim of learning and providing a voice and opportunities for change?

Mental health

Most large organizations invest in supporting good wellbeing and put in place initiatives to make sure good wellbeing is promoted. For example, Mental Health First Aiders, employee assistance initiatives, gym membership and so on.

- Do you have specific provisions and individuals that are able to support those who experience racism, bias and discrimination? This can include training your Mental Health First-Aiders in racism and its impact to allow them to better support Black and Brown people for example. It can also include acknowledging the link to intersectionality in your race equity work.
- Do you provide opportunities and create space for people of colour to share their experiences and connect with others, if they wish to.

Avoid

- Asking Black and Brown people if they racially code-switch. This is a sensitive, complex and nuanced element of racism.
- Adopting a colour-blind approach to situations, but rather, recognize differences and similarities and the diversity that people bring with them.
- Assuming all people of colour have the exact same experience.
- Assuming that Whiteness has no impact on your organization due to the implementation of diversity policies – Whiteness is all pervasive.
- Feeling guilt, this is not about wanting White people to feel guilt, this is about using your energy to create positive change to move forward.

2

THE BLAME GAME

Aseia Rafique

Introduction

Lurking round the corner and in the back (or, for some people, the front) of our minds, there is always someone to blame. That person is the 'immigrant' or the 'asylum seeker', the Muslim or the trans woman. The 'other', as these people have come to be defined, are 'not one of us', but (and essentially) they are at once both present and absent in our lives, and in the structures around us. For example, as Afua Hirsch points out in her work *Brit(ish)*: 'I am the eternal outsider... race is something unseen, unspoken of and unacknowledged in polite society.'[1] At the same time, Black and Brown people are visible by their very Blackness and otherness. And, as has happened many times before, they are forcing others to see them, to see their lives, to see their struggle. Black Lives Matter, as mentioned in Chapter 1, tore at the fissure of 'polite society', pulling all of us into a conversation about race, blame, history and consequences. 'Whose fault is it?' – that perennial question sitting silently in the back of people's minds. And what, in fact, can we do about it?

Race is a tricky concept. Its presence and absence can be difficult to define, existing in a framework of how we firstly identify ourselves and then how we relate to and identify with others. As a socially or self-defined construct, race can be anything we want it to be, but biologically and by virtue of being the same species, we know that all human beings are 99.9 per cent identical in their genetic make-up. Differences in the remaining 0.1 per cent simply hold important clues about the causes of diseases. So, if we are genetically so similar, why do some (or many) of us have a problem with race? Why are Black and Brown people so often denigrated and passed over in favour of Whiteness? What we do know is that race, like binary gender, is visible and noticeable. Pretending it does not exist, or that colour is a myth, is a fallacy some people prefer. It is a kind of 'get out clause' – 'I'm not racist, because I don't see colour'. In my opinion, it is easier to do that than to face up to or acknowledge that Black and Brown people face discrimination and have to constantly transact with bias in their everyday lives.

A look back in time

Bias and racism have been around for centuries and to understand the toxicity of what it presents, we need to go back and take a look at what history tells us. History is powerful and frightening, because it reveals the struggles of oppression and powerful in what it reveals – conquest, colonialism and colonization. Slavery, for example, in place for over 400 years, shows it is not easy to divorce the wealth of nations from those forced to create it. And this 400-year legacy remains with us – we continue to use many phrases associated with such oppression today – the most common one being 'divide and rule' – an expression still with us today. I hear it in conversations with family and friends and, oddly enough, even in the workplace. And words from other nations are mingled with our own: monsoon, purdah, chutney, bandana – dungarees even! My White Scottish father-in-law recognized the word jaldi (meaning hurry up) from his own background when I was shouting at the family one year to hurry up or we would be late for a family Eid dinner.

History is all around us and powerful in that it provides context to the struggles and demands of both minority and majority groups. It is complicated and complex, and although we might wish to demarcate history into 'good' or 'bad', into binary opposites, we can't. What we should do is to try and share, as far as we are able, all of our histories. Attempts to deny or distort history have been around for as long as history itself, but to allow this distortion of history is not only unhelpful but denies the true consequences and impact of what has come before. Shared learning can contextualize and help create meaningful change against racism and racist attitudes. However, when it becomes a battle over who is right or wrong and lines are drawn in the sand, then we have all lost. Even arguments about whether something as momentous as the existence of the Holocaust occur, even though it is one of the most well-documented events in history. If we use the power of history and tell all of it, rather than blaming everything on one or other group of people, we can help educate and learn about the complexities of historical events and move away from 'being triggered', a phrase aimed at those getting upset with people trying to reduce racism and racist attitudes. History is powerful because it can be used to break down the barriers of division but only if we tell it and only if we teach it. I didn't learn about Black or Brown history at school or about colonialism or about why Commonwealth countries exist. Later learning about the partition of India, I was shocked to discover how little I knew and how huge a role the British played in their occupation of India. We all need to know about this and other similar events, and not just those of us who are Black or Brown.

I feel that Britain, or at least a particular section of it, refuses to recognize the role it played or perhaps at the very least believes it is privileged enough not to have to face up to its past crimes and injustices. It is particularly good at obfuscation, pretending that as a country, we are fair and just, or that we are simply better than other countries, and isn't that enough? After all, as the aphorism goes, when two or three British people are gathered together, they form a queue. But in richer, more egalitarian countries like Germany or Sweden, Britain is viewed as being one of the more unequal societies because of the gap between rich and poor and because of the link between wealth and education. This, I believe, is one of the reasons why we have been unable to frame and reveal the racism and bias experienced by Black and Brown people. Politicians glorify the past, take pride in our kings and queens, but refuse to acknowledge Britain's role in the more unpalatable parts of history. The problem is that the repercussions of that history continue to unfold around us today. Instead of interrogating our history, we are told instead to admire our democracy, our 'British values', our egalitarian society and put aside personal animosities and ideological differences. It's where we are now that matters, isn't it? But where we are now feels as if Britain is working as a kind of fiction, the conceit being that in some way it represents and has the best interests of each of us at heart. It pretends it is inclusive and asks us to suspend our disbelief when we come across bias, discrimination or racism – the point being that we experience this as individuals, between one person and another. This individual, person-to-person prejudice takes away the blame from institutions. It insinuates that biased behaviour is my own fault and not influenced by those around me. As the previous chapter explains, it is the sheer Whiteness of institutions that can impact on Black and Brown people and are not necessarily isolated incidents of racism. But just as we tend to blame the poor for not working hard enough, for not being able to pull themselves out of poverty and most of all for being 'lazy and feckless', similarly, our collective response to racism does not randomly arise out of a vacuum but is created and reinforced by stories told by people in power, which reinforce the required White-dominant narrative.

We also know that the past is not just one group of people pitting themselves against another. It is the benefits – economic, social or other advantages that people procure over others. And inevitably there will always be people buying into the oppression of their own communities – whether for power, privilege, wealth or personal protectionism. As David Olusoga narrates in *Black and British: A Forgotten History*, African slaves were brought inland to Bunce Island, an island where slaves were held before being traded on river canoes: 'Some of these traders were Africans, others were from mixed race Afro-Portuguese or Afro-English.'[2] And history, colonial or otherwise, is littered with 'betrayals' – we have the Anglo-Sikh Wars of 1845 and 1848, when Sikh generals 'betrayed' their own army and changed the course of history – but for which historian Amarpal Singh Sidhu[3] believes 'Pakistan would have never been in existence.'[4] Bias and racism is not a battle between two halves – between those of us who are White and those of us who are Brown or Black – it is present across communities and societies. However, the dominance of Whiteness in creating wealth, privilege and power at the expense of minority communities has created deep-seated inequalities with which we are all still coming to terms.

We cannot go round in circles blaming one another, but we should acknowledge the part we play and continue to play in the oppression of others. And this is where knowledge, understanding and acceptance can replace stereotypes and bigotry. Throwaway statements, such as those ubiquitous and often-shared opinions on social media – here is one I read recently: 'see that over there! It's the Airport. If you don't like our country and its history, use It!' (sic) – shows not only a lack of understanding but an act of aggression against Black and Brown people who are asking for access to a meritocracy, to opportunities and to equality of outcomes in line with their White peers. What we don't need more of is to play the blame game and to split people's loyalties over who they are and where they belong. As visible Brown people we cannot (and should not have to) 'know our place' or 'stay in our lane'. Visiting and even living in the country from which parents and grandparents emigrated does not necessarily equate with 'home' – 'we are as different there as we are here'. As Akala sets out in his book *Natives: Race and Class in the Ruins of Empire*, a common question which almost always gets thrown around (with echoes of the social media comment I referenced above) is: 'why don't you go back home?'[5] I often always wonder where racist White people who complain think we should go? This *is* home, and for many of us there is nowhere else to go. Some Black and Brown families have been living in Britain for four generations or more. Michael Boyle, in an article he wrote for the *Guardian*, explained that his great-grandparents came to Britain in the 1800s, but as a Black man he is still made to feel he does not belong. Why is this? To put it bluntly, it is because the colour of your skin matters. The lighter you are, the more accepted; the darker you are, the less accepted. Whiteness has been normalized as the desired shade to be, as seen, for example, by the proliferation of the skin-whitening industry. We might think that such emphasis on skin colour, rather than intelligence or kindness, is madness, and it is. But for some people the need to feel superior to others must be how they feel better about themselves. Recently, a parent mentioned to me about how her four-year old child was excluded from a birthday party because he is Black. This is cruelty, but such examples, unfortunately, remain commonplace and such demarcations happen across the world, and from my experience and observations, mainly on the grounds of race and religion. If we look further afield to India, for example, it has been held together by its constitution, which promises equality to all, but now with the Prime Minister Narendra Modi's Bharatiya Janata Party on the rise, some people are beginning to count as more Indian (Hindus) than others (Muslims). All of us can read about or observe first-hand inequality and racist attitudes taking hold, whether that is because of religion or belief, the colour of someone's skin or any other irrelevant factor, and we can see that politics is pivotal to creating a fairer, more just world. But as so often happens, deep-rooted, racist attitudes are hard to change, helping to preserve superiority over others and generate injustice, inequality and difference. However, in Britain today more Black and Brown people are sharing their stories, as it is no longer acceptable to be seen as 'less' than compared to White people. Furthermore, sharing personal histories and data highlighting inequalities in employment and other areas helps to support a better understanding of the reasons why some Black and Brown people are being more and more vocal. Even on a trip to Pakistan, where I was delighted to see that I blended in, by colour at least, as soon as I spoke, it was obvious by my accent that I was not a resident. And annoyingly, as soon as I spoke, out came bottles of Coke and questions about where I actually lived and, sometimes even, whether I would be able to lend a helping hand to the latest business ventures some had on the go. I have been told by strangers and even acquaintances that I don't fit in here in Britain, and equally that I don't fit in in the country of my mother's birth, Pakistan. There are millions of Black and Brown people who straddle two or more worlds, living as part of a diaspora in countries to which parents, grandparents and great grandparents migrated. I have also been told, as well as picked up from not so subtle conversations, that Brown and Black people should support and make better (and of course go and live) in the countries of their heritage to make them less of a 'shithole' country, to quote a remark made by Donald Trump as President of the United States in 2018 when referring to the African countries of Haiti and El Salvador. One of the reasons for problems and challenges encountered by these so-called 'shithole' countries is colonization and the development of Western countries at the expense of poorer nations. The power of debt, held over developing countries, as well as the politics of war, conflict and resources has meant some countries have not been able to develop and expand as they may have liked to. Racists think Black and Brown people 'flood' to Britain to take away money and resources from British people. But the historical context of migration, as mentioned earlier, is much more complex. And why shouldn't I as a Brown person live my life in the best way, just as it is afforded to a White person?

Acknowledging our part in history is not just about reckoning with the past. And it is not just about honing in on one aspect of it – race – as the culture wars we are seeing seem to suggest it is. We conveniently forget that race also intersects across class inequalities and disadvantage too. Living in poverty affects people of all colours and the division created by such dominant narratives as 'White working-class boys' in direct conflict and opposition to Black working-class boys, for example, is as unhelpful as it is divisive. Although poverty separates and divides, the colour of a person's skin is an additional factor that negatively affects Black and Brown people and their families and often moves to affect future generations as well.

Acknowledging Britain's past is something the recently published government report on racism did not do very well. The *Sewell Report* from the Commission on Race and Ethnic Disparities[6] itself whitewashed the history and context of race inequality and had a worryingly positive tone towards colonialism. Lady Doreen Lawrence warned that the report risks pushing the fight against racism 'back twenty years or more.'[7] An acknowledgement of structural racism in Britain is needed to help us all to better understand how we can improve and make changes. We already know the changes that are needed, but if we continue to deny the existence of institutional racism in Britain, and we continue to promote the idea that an individual is at fault for any disadvantage they happen to experience, and we continue to overlook structural inequalities – all endorsed at the highest level in government – then we will continue to minimize the experiences of minorities living in Britain today. This is not simply about 'pulling up your bootstraps' and 'getting on with it', but identifying how structural inequity negatively impacts the lives people are living today, explored in more detail in Chapter 3.

Culture wars

This tension between cultures continues to play out as much today as it has done previously. It is shameful to note, for example, that

Asian-Americans (identified as Asians from countries such as China, Japan and Korea) continue to experience ongoing hate crimes. Those committing such atrocities – some of which have resulted in actual deaths – are being predominantly perpetrated by Black Americans. Two communities at risk from discrimination and harassment pitted against one another. Why is this? Is it just human nature and that people simply cannot get on with others? Looking a bit deeper we see communities who have been housed in poor neighbourhoods with scarce resources and few opportunities for employment. The competition for jobs and housing in this instance has led to animosity and separation between cultures and Black and Brown people.

This history of prejudice against Chinese Asians has played out before, perpetuated by various governments, with such ramifications resulting in further bias and discrimination today. Chinese Asians specifically were barred entry to the US in 1875, the country's first restriction on immigration, and again in 1882. The Chinese Exclusion Act barred Chinese labourers as part of the 1924 Immigration Act, which put a stop to Asian immigration. As Kenan Malik, a British writer explains, 'there is a deep and sordid history of bigotry'.[8] Racism is not a vacuum; history contributes, endorses and feeds into the narratives we see around us today. When immigration opened up to Chinese people some forty years later, they were housed in neighbourhoods already deprived and experiencing poverty. That tensions rose between Black and Chinese communities and that they are still being felt today is an indictment of political ill will.

Migration to Britain – and across the world – is not accidental and happens, not as some people believe just because of conflict or war, or the ineptitude or corruption of other countries' govern-ments, but also because of economics, finances and labour. The UK Government, for example, invited Black and Brown people to come and work in Britain, a policy which has criss-crossed generations. The arrival of migrants into Britain has a long and powerful history attached to it and is not simply a thought or flight of fancy that people living abroad thought they would travel to Britain one day. In some African schools, children were taught that they were British and taught to sing the British national anthem. 'Being British' was exported across the world, but for White people it became an issue when Black and Brown people then came to settle in Britain. The National Health Service (NHS) has used migrants since its inception in 1948, and the history of the NHS is also a history of economic migration. The shortfall of staff was met then, even as it is now, by 'importing' nurses, doctors and medical staff from overseas. As early as 1949, Britain led recruitment campaigns that resulted in thousands of nurses arriving in Britain from Malaysia, Mauritius and other parts of the Empire.[9]

Race becomes an issue when it is formulated as an issue, and government and politicians take the lead on how it is framed. As a child, I constantly heard my parents talk about how Britain worked, how its set up was to 'divide and rule' and Britain's role in the partition of India. And, importantly for them, how we children should not trust what was being told to us by White people, including by our educators. It turns out that in some respects they were right. Decolonizing the curriculum has gained greater traction in higher education in recent years, but government guidelines remain absent to encourage such change. In fact, there is growing dissent amongst some politicians that anything needs to be changed at all. The absence of lessons on Black and Brown history, instead helps detractors believe that Black and Brown people are the problem, and the reasoning behind why, for example, some statues should come down or place names renamed, or even the fact that historians are looking to provide a comprehensive understanding of Britain's link to colonization through art and culture, is met with horror by some. The issue becomes one about the stories that are worth telling, about who is telling those stories and about the images and representations that come to define us and dominate our lives.

My father, a bus driver, arrived a year after the Bristol Bus

Boycott of 1963. This bus boycott arose from the refusal of the Bristol Omnibus Company to employ Black or Asian bus drivers. As in other British cities at the time, there was widespread racial discrimination in housing and employment against the 'Coloureds' and this was one of the first Black-led campaigns against racial discrimination in employment.

A few years after the Bristol protests, a local dispute erupted in Wolverhampton when, in 1968, Sikh men protested against a ban on wearing turbans as bus drivers or working for the buses. Tarsem Singh Sandhu – a Punjabi bus driver in Wolverhampton – was sent home for choosing to wear both a turban and a beard. And he was around to hear Enoch Powell, MP for Wolverhampton South, describing the turban dispute as 'a cloud no bigger than a man's hand that can so rapidly overcast the sky'[10]. During the British Raj, Sikhs wore turbans while fighting for Britain during World War I and World War II. They wanted to wear one now. They organized a march through Wolverhampton which drew 6,000 Sikhs from across the country, demanding the lifting of the turban ban. The ban was lifted a year later, on 9 April 1969.

As World War II ended, Britain needed labour. The solution was to welcome migrants like my father and, as the poverty and persecution of independence took its toll, more and more economic migrants found their way to Britain in search of that 'better life'. The Black Country, in particular, benefitted from the new labour force and Asian people settled in towns such as Smethwick, West Bromwich and Wolverhampton. Families like mine arrived in the 1960s, including those who had been established and living wealthy and successful lives in East Africa – in countries like Uganda, which had its own violent issues of bias and discrimination that it pushed so mercilessly onto its citizens. The brutality and ethnic cleansing of the Idi Amin era is well documented. Amin, known as the 'Butcher of Uganda', was considered one of the cruellest despots in world history. Asian migration at this time followed the independence of these countries, with many moving for jobs, stability and some because of persecution.

And we saw in Chapter 1 how a racist slogan was the basis for Smethwick MP Peter Griffiths's election campaign. This was the backdrop to immigrant lives in Britain. My father arrived just in time to witness Griffiths's campaign succeed in mobilizing racist working-class sentiment. And although my father was not there to meet Malcolm X, he heard news of him coming to Smethwick in 1965. Malcolm X walked down Marshall Street, where White residents had campaigned for houses to be bought by the Tory council so they could let them to White families only.

As a young man in Kenya, my father was looking to qualify as a draughtsman. Already working at a British firm, he felt this experience would enable him to follow a career in Britain if he so chose. But as firms began to close and British companies began to withdraw from their offices abroad, the job market took a nosedive. My father's uncle, already living in the UK, encouraged him to seek a new life abroad.

When he first arrived, and just like immigrants before him, my father found himself renting a room with ten other Asian men for £1 a week. He began work in the local steel factory and two and a half years later joined Midland Red buses as a driver. The money was better, he said, but constantly being referred to as 'P*ki', or told that he smelled of garlic was less pleasant. He went on to rent a room in a house in Dudley with another Asian couple, and then a larger house, housing four Asian families. What is interesting is that houses were rented out by Asian landlords to Asian people, bypassing completely the 'No Irish, no Blacks, no dogs' sentiment of the day as also experienced by Vanisha's parents. And the discrimination did not stop at not being able to rent a room. For some Black and Brown people, they were discriminated against by financial institutions meaning they were not able to secure bank loans to buy property or other things they may have needed. This meant that for some members of the South Asian community, their contingency was to pool their money and lend to one another. Some founded 'committees', in which a group of people payed regular amounts into money-sharing pools and receiving the 'maximum amount' available when needed or when it was their turn. Extended families also supported each other to buy houses for cash, a practice which continues today, meaning that mortgages and paying interest to a financial institution is completely bypassed. In the US, a report from the Federal Reserve in 2017 showed that more than half of companies that have Black owners were turned down for loans, a rate twice as high as White business owners. This discrimination over loans and finance still holds unfortunately in many places even today.

The 1960s saw racist attitudes reach a new high with local politicians exploiting people's fears over housing and school shortages. But by the 1970s, immigration from Asia saw tens of thousands more people arrive. Navigating their way round this new life, my father knew he needed White friends. Having been befriended by the local Jehovah's Witnesses, he was keen to integrate. Such relationships helped when, having been caught in a fight with another man, both my parents were arrested and taken to the police station. The phone call to his White friend meant my father was able to use his 'White friend card' to get out of trouble. His friend spoke to the police officer and within minutes they were released. This was after being held at the police station for a few hours and which for my mother was a particularly distressing experience.

Men like my father, who went on to send for their wives to join them, had by now realized they were actively excluded from opportunities – excluded from jobs, housing and education. They had never been, even if they had thought so initially, on an equal footing with White men, and they knew it. Their male privilege, for so long nurtured in cultures and homes where they had been revered and pampered, dimmed and blotted under the glare of Whiteness. Without homes, they lived together in shared accommodation, washed and bathed at council-run swimming baths and tried to earn a living. And as they settled, they lived together, six or seven families at a time. Knowing no one, these families built up communities, set up businesses, drove taxis and worked at the local chicken factory down the road. They came at a time when labour was needed.

If you couldn't speak the language it was inevitably difficult to connect with White families living around and next to you. Black and Brown communities bonded because of their experience of being the 'other' in a country where racial slurs were heard every day. The comedian Shazia Mirza recently spoke about a racist experience from thirty years ago. Both her and her mum were getting on a packed train at Birmingham New Street when a White woman came on board, pushed her mum off the train and said, 'Get out the way you P*ki bastard!'[11] My parents also had similar experiences. My father tells me he was regularly spat at by White passengers when at work driving a bus. In areas of the Black Country, Asian communities began to settle, but they were not homogenous groups of people, with the same language and customs, although to the outside eye, the stereotypical phrase was that 'everyone looked – and smelled – the same'. To the outsider, it would have been perhaps impossible to identify that person from Lahore or that one from Mirpur or that one from Amritsar. Even Sikhs, a distinct group of Asians with a different religion, were bundled together as being the same. And with Islamophobia spiking, Sikhs continued to suffer the ignominy of being mistaken for Muslims – being exposed to hate crimes and Islamophobic attacks because of their brown skin, beards and turbans.

Through the looking glass – a peek at bias

People, it seems, are most comfortable looking introspectively at themselves, where in the privacy of their own thoughts they can acknowledge and frame their biases. We can, if we so wish, admit to having them and perhaps think carefully about not reinforcing them in the workplace or elsewhere. We can call out our biases in private and that's what matters, isn't it? Because anything and everything else is not our fault. The structures we feed into, the way systems are set up and the way workplaces are run, none of this is of our doing and changing systems and processes appears to be tricky and complex. Chapter 3 discusses such structural and systemic bias in the workplace. So if we continue to focus inwards, what happens outwards and elsewhere is someone else's problem, isn't it? The ever-popular and enduring Harvard Implicit Association tests,[12] which test for hidden biases, is one way in which we can self-improve. But what we need to supplement such tests with are tests that can evaluate and identify structural and systemic bias found in organizations and workplaces all over Britain. Employment, health, housing, educational inequalities and disparate outcomes in crime experienced by Black and Brown people exist for a reason.

I have come across many workplaces that are happy to virtue-signal and self-indulge when discussing or promoting the work they are doing on inclusion and equity. But this is without making the changes needed to have a lasting impact. We still, for example, have few women, disabled people, Black people, Asian people and others leading FTSE 100 companies because, when it comes down to it, it's hard to relinquish advantage. Both Vanisha and I are acutely aware of the lack of Black and Brown people in senior positions. Surely it should be about skills and experience when appointing people to the top and not about being Black or Brown. People that have advantage bring like-minded people to the table; they appoint like-minded people and, by simply doing nothing, continue to create disadvantage for others and retain advantage for themselves.

We are normalized into believing that change happens at a glacial pace, but it doesn't have to be like that. The pandemic, if nothing else, has shown that anything is possible. With many people working from home, the workplace was suddenly equalized for those whose personal circumstances meant they were unable to stay late at the office, or who found commuting to work a struggle, or for those with health needs who found that being at home meant they could work without having to experience pain. For some, it was the first time where they suddenly found themselves on an equal footing with others, having been granted access to people, training, events and resources in line with peers and colleagues.

It shouldn't be that complicated

What is it that makes it so complicated? We have the power to change things and people in power especially have the power to change things. But we are often derailed by interminable discussions about what is the 'right' thing to do. And having such discussions plays into the hands of those that do not want to see change, those that don't see why change is needed and those who are simply opposed to any kind of change. Trying to frame 'wokeism' and negate people's desire for change has become almost a crusade in itself. I remember a politician during the local elections of May 2021, making the remark that wokeness was well and truly alive, which shows what a firebrand the term 'woke' has become.

This fixation on 'wokeism' is all about division. Similarly with Brexit, the problem was remainers or 'remoaners' if you will, rather than leavers. We seem to be at our happiest blaming each other for either being too woke or having bias; but creating and constantly fanning the flames of blame means less attention is paid towards the things that matter and the political capital generated by this ultimately buys into the argument that says we don't need to make the society we live in fair and equitable, as it is working fine as it is. The concentration and current fixation on wokeness, on patriotism and monoculturalism has led to a denial of difference, and this obsession with wokeness and of having to be constantly socially aware, has turned 'wokeness' into a commodity. Wokeness turns people into clichés and caricatures (after all, it's easier to ignore or dismiss someone who's not 'real') and racism, sexism, homophobia or classism are met either with indifference or outrage. And being outraged at injustice or 'wokeness', plays into the hands of those who do not want to affect real change. 'Woke' is a term meaning 'alert to injustice in society, especially racism,'[13] or a vernacular term meaning conscious of one's own oppression. The word, now used pejoratively by those who identify as 'anti-woke', has meant it has become a hostile, bad-faith term. It has instead taken on the form of slogans: Black Lives Matter, Decolonize the Curriculum, Trans Women Are Women, Check Your Privilege and Educate Yourself, amongst others. But what we need to watch out for amid the constant disparagement of being woke is that we do not dismiss the opinions of others if they do not conform to our own. The collective pressure to do something, for example organizations releasing anti-racist statements, or individuals posting a black square on social media, has become overwhelming and in some respects stands in the way of any actual change happening. Such acts are simple virtue signalling because, from what I can see, very little emerges from it. Organizations that rushed to set out their commitments on anti-racism now languish, carefully composed, on a whiteboard at the back of an office.

The discussion and the pros and cons people have about workplace quotas and targets, for example, is endless. Those that didn't 'make it' or didn't progress in their careers as much as they felt they should have done are blamed for not trying hard enough, for not being good enough or for not having the 'right' skillset. The individual is to blame but not the gatekeepers. Rupi Kaur, an artist and poet, speaks about how proud she is that #rupikaurlive, is an independently produced and self-released film of her poems – 'just because the gatekeepers don't think there is a market for our stories doesn't mean we're going to stop telling them,'[14] she says. And quotas *can* work; they increase the representation of an under-represented group. Labour introduced all-women shortlists (AWS) intended to increase the proportion of female MPs in the UK and at the 1997 general election, 35 out of 38 Labour all-women shortlist candidates were elected. At the same time, those opposing such shortlists took the Labour Party to court for sex discrimination, so following the reduction in female MPs after the 2001 general election, Labour introduced the Sex Discrimination (Election Candidates) Act 2002, which remains in place until 2030 as part of the Equality Act 2010.

There has been many an argument saying quotas and targets are unnecessary while conveniently forgetting the structural inequalities and bias at play, limiting those from under-represented and diverse backgrounds from roles already taken up by those in power. People who are privileged by the system – who benefit from structural inequality – are less likely to notice or be bothered by it. Just imagine that if the current system worked and the right people were successfully recruited and promoted for the right jobs in ALL circumstances, what would we have? Certainly, there would not be so many leadership positions occupied by White middle-aged men.

The fallacy of meritocracy is set deep. We cannot imagine, or indeed hate to acknowledge, that some of our achievements are a result of parents who read to us, or a tutor who helps pass an exam or a place at private school. And it is anathema to suggest – or even think – that it wasn't just hard work that led us to that position of CEO, director, or even hedge fund manager. And this is where the waters muddy on quotas and targets. People do not want to feel they have been supported by others or by systems and structures that were put in place to help create opportunities. They do not want to think they were 'part of a programme' to help them achieve their goals. And those falling outside the remit of such support are vocal in their 'What about me? I need support too' responses. And quoting back at you are those who say: 'So-and-so made it, so why can't you?'

We need to watch out for the gatekeepers, those keen to keep the status quo and the reserve of privilege and power. This gatekeeping impacts on all marginalized groups and Black and Brown people who, without the right connections or networks, continue to struggle in the meritocracy we all believe is in place. And people desperately want to believe that it is their hard work that helps them make it – to such an extent that some go back generations to find that story of struggle that shows they haven't had it easy. Sam Friedman, a sociologist at the London School of Economics, and a commissioner at the government's Social Mobility Commission, found in their research[15] that 'individuals who believe most strongly that meritocracy is working are the ones that believe hard work is the key to success.' Their findings indicate that people tend to downplay their own, fairly privileged upbringings and instead find stories of the past – of working-class struggle, of upward social mobility, of meritocratic striving – for explaining their own experiences and identity and of having made it in the world, even if they do have to go back a couple of generations to find their 'struggle' stories.

Despite all the talk of meritocracy and social mobility, Britain, as Akala succinctly defines it, 'is still a society where the social class and area you are born into will determine much of your life experiences, chances and outcomes.'[16]

Fundamentally, as we discuss in our further chapters, it is the people in power who are the ones that can decide to look at the system and evaluate how it works. They can make the changes we need to see and put the focus on structural and systemic biases where it is needed.

The first time I was called P*ki

When I was first called a 'P*ki', it wasn't a surprise. It was a word I had already heard, a word I saw follow others as they walked down the street, as they met with friends or picked up children from school. I ignored it of course, carefully looking over my shoulder to be sure that whoever had shouted it wasn't actually following me. I was only a child myself – nine or ten. But what this casual racism did was to make me question what was right. Was it right that I ate roti most days, a round flatbread made with wheat flour, or should I have been eating, even in my own opinion, chips? And honestly, I love chips just as much as I enjoy eating roti. But as we internalize misogyny, so too do we similarly internalize White superiority, which can lead to racial code-switching, explored earlier in Chapter 1. It was only later, in my teenage years, that I started to question the meaning of such slurs and was surprised to find out that the word 'Pak' (pronounced paak) meant pure and clear. The irony, even now, is not lost on me.

But we threw insults around about others too. We didn't just accept that as an Asian Muslim family we were the 'outsiders' but, just as we had slurs thrown at us, we felt we could do the same to others. We felt we had the right to laugh at other people and make jokes about their culture or religion. This was, I am sure, so as to feel superior over others, just as others felt and reinforced their superiority over us. Oddly enough, the main recipient for bias in our Muslim family was Sikhism and I say 'oddly' because there is so much similarity between these two South Asian cultures – that there is not much to distinguish between them. There is the food, the geography, the language and the physical similarity of people originating from the region of Punjab – but not the religion, of course, which is perhaps where some of this animosity lies. Tensions also increased as partition literally drew a line across shared identities and culture. And as Muslims trimmed their bodily hair to remain 'clean and pure', baptized Sikhs grew theirs. The five pillars of Islam (declaration of faith, prayer, giving alms to the poor, fasting and pilgrimage) represented the foundations of Muslim life and the five Ks: Kesh (uncut hair), Kangha (comb), Kara (iron bangle), Kachera (undergarment) and Kirpan (dagger) of Sikhism were items that Guru Gobind Singh commanded Sikhs to wear at all times back in 1699. These similarities meant nothing and were in fact the source of jokes between the two cultures.

Among our neighbours, there was a large community of people from Mirpur, a region bordering onto Indian-administered Kashmir. Speaking with a local dialect and language, these village communities were looked down on by those arriving from the cities such as Islamabad, Lahore and Karachi. They were thought of by the city dwellers as uncultured and uneducated. But 'White flight' didn't distinguish between those who came from cities or villages. Its concern was only if you were the wrong colour.

Migration has never been far from the news agenda and 'White flight' is the suggestion that White people do not want to live in neighbourhoods where there is a high percentage of Black and Brown people living. Today certain neighbourhoods have been marked as the 'majority minority', with so many ethnic minority residents that their presence makes some White British people fearful or unwilling to live in such areas. In 2017, Donald Trump claimed that parts of London were 'no-go areas' which had been radicalized by Muslims. Although Trump's rhetoric is alarmist and said to create fear of the 'other', moving house is about wanting to live in 'better and more upmarket' neighbourhoods. Black and Brown communities live in some of the most deprived boroughs in Britain and, because of their colour and because of systemic discrimination and because of politics and history, many have found themselves living with poverty and violence. The perception from the far right and far left and from racists is that Black and Brown people are immoral, dishonest and unscrupulous and not fit to live next door to. When a Black or Brown person does well, has a good job, is a CEO and more, they are seen as an anomaly. The feeling I get from some people is that if that Black or Brown person 'made it', then why can't everyone else. But not everyone 'makes it' anyway, whatever that term might mean, whether that is having a lot of money, or a prestigious job, or a large house and being White, just means that some people have been afforded some advantages, for example, in general White people do not experience racism or microaggressions regularly, and that helps.

We began to see families who believed they were 'better' and 'more educated' move into White neighbourhoods and, as irony would have it, they themselves were then not accepted by more middle-class boroughs. It didn't matter that their children were given or provided with more English-sounding names, they were still Brown and therefore 'different'.

These differences within and between communities were manifested in deeply held conservative beliefs. Women and girls had to wear traditional Salwar Kameez, with a scarf over the head to cover their hair. This meant that the school uniform at my school was adapted to suit the style of the traditional South Asian dress, with a navy-blue Salwar Kameez worn by most girls. To wear anything different was to be seen as different and 'not one of us'. It was difficult being of a community but not from the community. Called Lahorees, we in turn were mocked for displaying slightly more liberal beliefs. But as more of the middle-class South Asian community dispersed, willing themselves and their families to 'do better', 'work harder' and 'fit in', other families threw themselves together, building close-knit communities, which also helped to shield them from the worst of racist attitudes.

What I cannot understand is why people hate so much or believe information about others without evaluating what is or isn't true. The need to abuse others because they look different or happen to wear religious clothing, for example, seems to elicit horror in some. But why can't we let people be? Whether you agree or not, that should not matter – you live your life, they live theirs.

It is only the binary that seems to matter, right and wrong, black and white. We continue to have the same conversation and ask the same questions: 'If you don't like it here, why don't you go back home?' As we saw in the previous chapter, Akala answers this and other similar questions in his chapter, 'Interlude: A Guide to Denial', from his book, *Natives: Race and Class in the Ruins of Empire*.[17] Ambalavaner Sivanandan expressed it as: 'We are here, because you were there.'[18] This binary world or dialectical oppositions such as mind/body, culture/nature, permeate our world and places such oppositions in conflict with each other. Where one is good, the other has to be bad. But bias is nuanced. And this goes unrecognized. Currently, the way in which we interact with bias is binary and simplistic.

As I stated earlier, it seems that it always has to be someone's fault; there is always someone to blame and more often than not it is the individual, and rarely the structure in which they find themselves. We are labelled as 'left' or 'right', but why can't we be both? Young Muslim teenage girls who ran away from home when I was growing up, were blamed by their family and then blamed again for having the audacity to want something better. They were blamed for becoming 'White'.

What I have noticed increasingly is that everything seems to be consigned to one of two things. You're either with us or you're not. You're right or you're wrong, or you're either woke or you're not. This obsession with the binary plays out everywhere, from interactions with friends to media articles and even to the very existence of social media and the platforms on which they sit. The very nature of the binary helps polarize discussion, pulling away at its complexity. Why won't anyone talk anymore and what makes it so difficult?

I have got used to reading the commentary on Twitter or Facebook or any of the other multiple platforms we use daily. I view these comments as little capsules of dislike and a projection of loathing and dislike for others' opinions. Everything elicits an opinion and there is a tacit agreement that I will be pitting my wits against yours and that I can hate more than you.

Growing up, this perception of right and wrong, black and white, you and me, was never so obvious as when I think about my mother. She was a young girl of nineteen when she left Lahore to join my father in England. Having left behind her parents, family and friends, she found herself newly married in a country in which she did not speak the language. Not being able to speak English defined my mother's existence in the UK. Access to healthcare, education and life outside the home was, in varying degrees, denied to her. And she felt this most acutely by White people telling her to learn the language of the country. These were sometimes well-meaning health workers who might point her in the direction of the local college, where she could take night classes or, perhaps, there were classes during the day she could take while the children were at school. And then there were the less well-meaning GPs who said she had been here long enough now, and she should be able to speak English. I know this because, as a little girl, I went with my mother to some of her appointments and as the 'official' translator, these messages were directed at me. I remember the looks, the quick glance in my direction before the eyes flitted away. Looks which spoke of disapproval and self-importance because who on earth would bring a child with them to translate for them?

What was difficult for my mother was not that she didn't want to know how to speak English or that she just wasn't intelligent enough to grasp another language, but the assumption that simply because she now lived in England, she should know and be familiar in its language, in its undulations, dialect and cultural nuances. But for my mother, and people like her, it turned out that life was not that simple. Her choice was not simply a binary one, where she could decide to either learn or not learn English. Her choices were restricted because of sexism and racism.

REFLECTIONS TO SUPPORT GOOD PRACTICE

- Have you taken the time to learn about the history of Black and Brown communities?
- Make a conscious effort not to judge someone based on the colour of their skin or the clothes they wear.
- Think about equality, diversity and inclusion in the organization you work in?
- Take the time to get to know people from different back-grounds and cultures.
- Take the time to understand the politics of race and racism.

- Think about the language you use. Try and be inclusive of others.
- Read multiple sources of news; make sure you look at different places and ways in which to get your information.

3

INSTITUTIONAL AND STRUCTURAL RACISM – JUST SAY IT!

Vanisha Parmar

> *I was taught to see racism only in individual acts of meanness, not in invisible systems conferring dominance on my group.*[1]
> Peggy McIntosh

I am writing this after the murder of George Floyd and a few weeks following the verdict on Derek Chauvin. The dust seems to have settled and I sense some calm, perhaps even a sigh of relief and a moment to relax. This is my perception of how most people are feeling. By 'people', to be exact, I mean those who are in the positions of power and have the seniority and ability to influence making race equity a reality. These people are usually (not always) White.

Following the murder of George Floyd, I felt an immediate rise of panic in organizations, a feeling amongst senior leaders that more proactive action and targeted work should have been carried out to promote race and to address the disparities that most organizations see when reviewing their data. Equally, I sensed some nervousness amongst these organizations about being uncovered for the lack of progress they had made. No one quite knew what was going to happen as a result of George Floyd's death, but the global wave of condemnation was most certainly a sign that perhaps something significant was in the air.

I don't think the pangs of slight anxiety organizations were experiencing were out of genuine remorse for most organizations and very senior people in those organizations, but more out of being exposed. Being exposed for the lack of effort and commitment that had been put into the race agenda; rather like how one might feel when a concealed lie is just about to be exposed. I didn't get this sense from any conversation directly, but it was my observation. Organizations were now worried about what their data was showing and hurriedly coming up with a narrative for that data accompanied with a list of actions that they could share internally with their staff and externally should they need to. This might feel like a positive outcome, but my view is that this superficial, knee-jerk approach brings no longevity. I now see some organizations backtracking from the actions and initiatives they committed to at the time for one reason or another. This is not to say that within these large organizations there are not some very good, genuinely committed individuals and allies who want to achieve equity; however, a few good individuals are not enough to address years of racial inequality in organizations. Following George Floyd, the world was watching, and activists, think-tanks and protestors were all asking the same question: Why, some fifty years on since race equality legislation in the UK have we failed to make progress?

Race in organizations

In the publication 'Race in the Workplace – The McGregor-Smith Review',[2] Smith states: 'We should live in a country where every person, regardless of their ethnicity or background, is able to fulfil their potential at work. Sadly, I feel we are still a long way from this'.[3]

We were a long way from this when the murder of Stephen Lawrence took place, and we are still a long way away in 2022. For most large organizations, race equality has always been on the agenda; however, when it comes to the myriad inequalities that must be addressed, race equity seems to be much further down on the list of priorities. This view is shared by so many Black and Brown people I have talked to. Organizations seem much more at ease with responding to the challenges and disparities around gender and LGBTQ+ than they ever have been with race. Race is often cited as an uncomfortable and sensitive topic, but for me, this is a White-centric view. White people find it uncomfortable to talk about racism perhaps more than race and this is one of the contributory factors to the lack of progress. I must mention, this has not been due to lack of trying by diversity practitioners, allies staff networks and some senior leaders – however, as I previously mentioned, a few good people will not amount to the progress that is required.

The racially motivated murder of the Black British teenager Stephen Lawrence in 1993 and the subsequent Macpherson Report following the investigation on the handling of the incident in 1999, exposed the way in which racism operated at an institutional and organizational level. The late Sir William Macpherson's report[4] concluded that the Metropolitan Police's investigation into the murder of Stephen Lawrence had been 'marred by a combination of professional incompetence, institutional racism and a failure of leadership by senior officers.'[5] It made seventy recommendations and found that institutional racism extended beyond the Metropolitan Police Service. This was a real opportunity to address some of the deep-rooted structural racism that leads to unfair treatment and differential outcomes for Black and Brown people that we still see in so many aspects of society today.

It was a significant moment for race in the UK and, for the first time, I felt that the culpability had shifted from individual acts of racism to recognizing and acknowledging the historical role that institutions and collective powers played in perpetuating racism, Whiteness and White supremacy. The changes in race equality legislation following Stephen Lawrence meant that it was no longer sufficient to react to discrimination when it occurred; instead, there was a requirement on organizations to implement measures to prevent discrimination from arising in the first place. This was exactly what was needed: a systematic and thorough approach to tackling racial inequality with some accountability to make it happen. For me this felt like light at the end of the tunnel; finally, there was a legal requirement to take proactive action. Sadly however, for some organizations this was burdensome and unnecessary and the changes to the Equality Act 2010 as a result of the Red Tape Challenge in 2011[6] (put forward by the coalition government) to reduce the overall burden of regulation were very much welcomed by many. The Red Tape Challenge was a review of regulations that the government at the time inherited with the aim of reducing them as much as possible. The government committed by the end of 2013 to scrapping or improving at least 3,000 regulations through this initiative.[7] The changes led to some of the requirements of equality legislation, in particular in relation to the public sector equality duty (requiring public bodies to approach addressing inequality and differential impact in policy and decision-making in a more robust and systematic way than had ever been required previously), being relaxed. With no real national authoritative watchdog and so few challenging large organizations, the foot really was off the gas and accountability absent on the race equity front. Most organizations were and still are doing very little to create equity for Black and Brown people.

I know that there are organizations that do put resources into promoting race equality and want to see some change – however, for some the impetus is usually stakeholder pressure and wanting to be seen to be doing the 'right' thing. The lack of progress to date for Black and Brown people is a clear indicator that when there is a shallow emphasis, and a desire for wanting to be *seen* to be doing the right thing, it does not lead to meaningful and tangible outcomes. Great sentiments are easily written and spoken;

however, it is the action taken and outcomes achieved that show a real level of commitment exists. Despite the resources put into the race equality agenda there is still no great progress and inequality persists. Some examples include:

- Black men are three times more likely to be arrested than White men.[8]

- Between 2008–9 and 2018–19, Black people accounted for 8 per cent of the UK deaths in police custody, while only making up 3 per cent of the total population.[9]

- Black people are almost four times more likely than White people in Britain to be in prison.[10]

- Nearly half (49 per cent) of FTSE 100 companies still lack any Black, Asian and minority ethnic representation at board level.[11]

- Only 9.8 per cent of FTSE 100 board members are from Black, Asian and minority ethnic backgrounds, of these ninety-nine BAME directors, 38.4 per cent are female; however, no Black, Asian and minority ethnic woman holds an executive job.[12]

- The most recent student data for the UK (looking at graduates of 2017–18) shows that the attainment gap is 13.2 per cent.[13]

- African-Caribbean people are three to five times more likely to be diagnosed and admitted to hospital for schizophrenia, more than any other group.[14]

- Black people were more than four times as likely as White people to be detained under the Mental Health Act.[15]

- Risk of dying among those diagnosed with COVID-19 is higher from those in Black, Asian and minority ethnic groups than in White ethnic groups.[16]

- Fewer than one in ten voluntary sector employees (9 per cent) are from Black, Asian and minority ethnic groups, a lower proportion than both the public and private sectors (both at 11 per cent) and a lower proportion than the UK as a whole (14 per cent).[17]

- In respect to charity boards, the Charity Commission's 2017 research into board effectiveness found that 92 per cent of all charity trustees were White and only 9.6 per cent of trustees in the top 100 charities by income are from a Black, Asian and minority ethnic background.[18]

- Black women are five times and Asian women two times more likely to die because of complications in pregnancy than White women.[19]

There are many more examples and subsequent reports explaining the reasons for these anomalies. In my view, although somewhat simplistic, they all boil down to institutional and structural racism. It is a direct unfavourable view; however, I want to cut through the gloss, the positive spins, the excuses and justifications for these disparities that leave Black and Brown people worse off. There seems to be a huge reluctance to address and accept racism in its raw, unapologetic form.

George Floyd

In the week of George Floyd's murder, I distinctly remember a particular conversation with two individuals. The murder took place on 25 May 2020 and the disturbing details unravelled in the subsequent days. It was well covered on all social media platforms and the video footage of Derek Chauvin, the police officer who knelt on George Floyd's neck for over nine minutes was spreading fast; it was everywhere. On 1 June 2020 – I remember this date as it was the first day back at work following a bank holiday over which the news of George Floyd's death was being uncovered at rapid pace – I joined a virtual conversation part-way through; the discussion was about the news and I was asked if I had watched it. I assumed, of course, they were talking about George Floyd and I was ready to launch in with my expressions of disgust and sadness. However, far from it – they were in fact talking about IKEA reopening after lockdown, and the huge queues that had been reported on TV. I was massively taken aback and shocked, not least because I had perceived them to be great allies with an excellent understanding of racial inequality. I am sure they don't remember this conversation; however, for me it was a poignant moment. It was a roaring reminder that there was a lack of concern immersed in privilege; even when it meant life and death. The murder of George Floyd didn't touch or affect them and, in that moment, Ikea trumped George Floyd. And in other circumstances, LGBTQ+ trumps race, gender equality targets trump race equality targets, and so on, forgetting that race is equally important and adopting this hierarchical approach perhaps unwittingly, serves no one. Tackling issues of race discrimination is just as important as addressing gender inequalities and the problems faced by the LGBTQ+ community for example.

Following George Floyd's murder there has most certainly been a shift towards a more open dialogue than there had been previously, and these discussions are very different to those I was engaging in five to ten years ago. I accept that since the murder of George Floyd there has been a flurry and volume of work being carried out by organizations. As I mentioned before, in a rush of panic, guilt or perhaps even genuine remorse and desire to want to do more, there has been a great push in wanting to be seen to be addressing racial inequality. Racism is a global reality and the international recognition that discrimination exists on many levels, to the point of death, is a rude awakening that can no longer be ignored.

The discourse that has taken place of late has mainly been centred around White privilege, White fragility, anti-racism and unconscious bias. However, these are not neoteric concepts, albeit they seem to have resurrected as vogueish terms that must be included to gain validity in discussions about race. For me, some of these discussions are a palatable deflection from talking about the core of the problem that exists: racism, in particular, structural and institutional racism and Whiteness. It is important to understand that this is central to the discussions we *need* to be having. I am not arguing that those concepts are not important, but they do not *replace* the discussion about racism. Racism, in all its forms, is the nucleus of which other nuances such as bias, prejudice, privilege form around. Superficial and empty conversations about race that do not address racism and institutional and structural racism honestly will not help us to achieve equity. Particularly when we are not talking about the root cause of many of the disparities that exist. You cannot kill a tree by trimming its branches; you must remove the root to stop it from growing ever again.

The dirty 'R' word

Before I get into a discussion about racism, I want to be clear about definitions, so we are at the same starting point. Often racism and its related terms are used interchangeably, however, they can mean very different things.

Racism

'Racism' consists of conduct or words or practices which advantage or disadvantage people because of their colour, culture or ethnic origin. In its more subtle form, it is as damaging as in its overt form.[20]

This definition is taken from the Stephen Lawrence Inquiry, published in 1999.[21] The last sentence is the operative one and the one that affects people of colour the most. It is this racism that takes places in organizations daily through the structures built by those in senior positions currently and before them. The word 'practices' refers to structures including policies, processes, procedures: everything that allows an organization to function and operate.

Institutional racism

Institutional racism relates to how organizations practice racism through their structures, policies, processes and functions. It was defined by Sir William Macpherson in the Stephen Lawrence Inquiry as:

> ...the collective failure of an organization to provide an appropriate and professional service to people because of the colour, culture or ethnic origin. It can be seen or detected in processes, attitudes and behaviour which amount to discrimination through unwitting prejudice ignorance thoughtlessness and racist stereotyping which disadvantage minority ethnic people.[22]

Structural racism

Structural racism operates at a macro-societal level, feeding into all aspects of society collectively via social, political and economic systems. According to Kehinde Andrews, 'It is how large-scale systems, historic and contemporary ideologies, social forces and processes combine and manifest in inequality between racial groups.'[23]

He adds: 'Structural racism refers to the systematic oppression of ethnic minorities that leads the disparities that we see in terms of income, employment, health etc.'[24]

White supremacy

White supremacy is the subtle way in which Whiteness is deemed to be the standard by which everything is judged and it permeates the way in which society is organized; it is superior. It extends to 'how systems and institutions are structured to uphold this White dominance.'[25]

I use the table below for easier reference and understanding.

Figure 1

RACISM	INSTITUTIONAL RACISM	STRUCTURAL RACISM	WHITENESS/ WHITE SUPREMACY
Conduct or words or practices which advantage or disadvantage people because of their colour, culture or ethnic origin. 'Racism is the systemised oppression of one race by another.'[26]	The way in which racism is embedded in an organization's structures, policies, processes and functions.	Operates societal level, feeding into all aspects of society collectively via social, political and economic systems. Structural racism refers to the systematic oppression of ethnic minorities that leads the disparities that we see in terms of income, employment, health etc.[27]	An ideology that is based on the belief that White people are superior in many ways. It describes the culture where White and everything associated with them (Whiteness) as the ideal standard.[28]

Usually, overt acts of racism will be accompanied by vocal reactions of disgust. And although some might think this is less of a problem, especially in organizations, overt racism still occurs in the working and professional environment. The Trades Union Congress (TUC) in 'An analysis of the 2016-2017 Trade Union Congress Racism at Work Survey'[29] reported that over 70 per cent of Asian and Black employees who took part in their survey experienced racial harassment at work. And in 2020 it was revealed that a former partner at a London law firm pulled a white A4 envelope over his head and joked to a Black member of staff, he had 'joined the Ku Klux Klan!'[30]

Shocking indeed, and I am certain that up and down the country there will be many that were horrified by such an act. This supports the comfortable narrative that 'true racism only exists in the hearts of evil people',[31] and the majority of us are not evil. I find that even when I have broached the subject of institutional racism tentatively it's produced a response that suggests 'How could you?' or 'How dare you make such accusations?'[32] In contrast, the subtle forms of racism that exist are overlooked, ignored and accepted as the norm. Why is this? Reni Eddo-Lodge[33] suggests that people think if there hasn't been an overt act of racism then racism hasn't occurred. The individual acts allow us to point a finger at someone or some specific group, absolving everyone else of any responsibility or accountability to look within and wider. The overt type of racism does not threaten a position of power, making it easier to point from the ivory tower.

DiAngelo states that racism is a system where the ideas of that system are reinforced in all aspects of society. 'From birth we are conditioned into accepting and not questioning these ideas. Ideology is reinforced across society... in schools, textbooks, political speeches, movies... words and phrases.'[34] This becomes accepted as the norm and leads to the subtle forms that take place at an institutional and structural level. James Boggs and Grace Lee Boggs in their paper 'Racism and the Class Struggle'[35] state:

...the various forms of oppression within every sphere of social relations-economic exploitation... political subordination, cultural devaluation... verbal abuse etc together make up a whole of interreacting and developing processes which operate so normally and naturally and are so much a part of the existing institutions of the society that the individuals involved are barely conscious of their operation.[36]

DiAngelo[37] claims that this racism is a structure of oppression that goes well beyond individuals. She explains that oppression occurs when prejudice is backed by legal authority and institutional control. 'This authority and control transform individual prejudices into a far-reaching system that no longer depend on the good intentions of individual actors; it becomes the default of the society and is reproduced automatically.'[38]

Not only are individuals not so conscious (apart from those who now might refer to themselves as 'woke') they are a part of the problem. Ijeoma Olua in her book *So You Want to Talk About Race* states that 'race was not only created to justify a racially exploitative economic system; it was invented to lock people of colour into the bottom of it.'[39] She suggests this then results in more 'profit' for people of colour who are deemed as superior and a feeling that those who are superior and a feeling that 'you will get more because they exist to get less'.[40]

When most organizations speak on race equality, it seems to be watered down, only dealing with the superficial aspects that do not quite get into it. Perhaps this is so as not to offend or make anyone feel uncomfortable. Not many talk in terms of oppression and Whiteness. To take the lid off racism would require White people to look at themselves, to accept and acknowledge that the existing structure benefits them and while it could be argued that since George Floyd this has started to take place, it also required action – to do something about it that go beyond one-off actions. I appreciate however, that it can be difficult to have a desire to dismantle something that benefits you and yours. DiAngelo[41] provides some explanations, she suggests there is an existence of White solidarity – an agreement amongst White people to protect their advantage and privilege and 'not cause another white person to feel racial discomfort.'[42] It requires silence, often referred to as 'White silence' to not expose the system of advantage and to remain united to protect supremacy. This resonates with me and I have often wondered whether the silence is broken in the higher echelons or whether it is just the unspoken rule of law that White people have become accustomed to as the norm.

I am certain there will be people who are reading this who will feel that I am being unfair. However, as I mentioned before, despite the volume of work (not always substance) towards achieving racial equality and equity the evidence suggests the equality of outcomes for Black and Brown people is yet to be achieved.

McGregor Smith's review published in 2017 states:

> For decades, successive governments and employers have professed their commitment to racial equality yet vast inequality continues to exist. This has to change now. With 14 per cent of the working age population coming from a Black or Minority Ethnic (BME) background, employers have got to take control and start making the most of talent, whatever their background.[43]

In the twenty years I have been working in the field of equality and diversity I have attended numerous events, talks and discussions; in addition, I have read many organizational reports. The theme that runs through all of them is that inequalities exist for people of colour whatever the sector; usually it's an underrepresentation of people of colour in the most senior positions, an attainment gap, an over-representation in disciplinaries or regulatory matters for some professions and so on. Some examples include:

- In the medical profession in the UK, Black, Asian and Minority Ethnic doctors are more likely to be referred to the UK regulator, the GMC (General Medical Council) by their employers or healthcare providers. BAME doctors have more than double the rate of being referred by an employer compared to White doctors.[44]

- When considering the contributions Black, Asian and Minority Ethnic groups make to our television programmes there is a lack of ethnic diversity across the majority of senior production roles compared to their representation in other roles, especially in junior and entry-level roles.[45]

- Just fifty-two out of the 1,099 most powerful roles in the country are filled by non-White individuals, or 4.7 per cent of the total number compared to the 13 per cent proportion of the UK population.[46]

- Black individuals in organizations are particularly under-represented, with just seventeen of the 1,099 roles held by Black men and women – amounting to 1.5 per cent compared to the national population figure of 3.6 per cent.[47]

- Out of more than 1,000 of the most senior posts in the UK, only 3.4 per cent of occupants were from BAME backgrounds.[48]

- There are no BAME Chief Constables and just one Police and Crime Commissioner; no CEOs and just three Chairs of the Top 50 NHS Trusts; no Permanent Secretaries in the Civil Service Board; no Supreme Court Judges; only one out of thirty-one Trade Union leaders; no CEO at the fifteen national sports governing bodies; and only five out of fifty Vice-Chancellors at the top fifty universities. In relation to businesses there are only two BAME FTSE 100 CEOs, only one advertising agency CEO, no CEOs at the top UK financial institutions, only six CEOs or Managing Partners at the UK's top sixty-one law, accountancy and consultancy firms.[49]

I know there are some organizations that work to understand the reasons behind the disparities that exist but I often wonder if there is an element of reticent and silent thinking amongst some White people that perhaps Black and Brown just aren't as good as White people; the cultures just don't allow them to prosper and perhaps the intellect is not on an equal par. Of course, this line of thinking, most popular in the nineteenth century, is somewhat unfavourable today – but I do wonder. Black and Brown people have demonstrated (and continue to demonstrate) their abilities and excellence in leadership and creativity in many fields, such as astronomy, engineering, mathematics, physics, economics, philosophy, medicine and politics; yet they fail to achieve at the highest echelons in the UK or even the West at large. Eddo-Lodge argues that the 'reasons for the lack of representation in different industries'[50] is not due to 'a lack of Black excellence, talent education, hard work or creativity. There are other, more sinister forces at play.'[51] These ominous forces are structural racism and Whiteness. Like me, most Black and Brown people who understand racism and how it operates will agree that the reasons for the above, at the simplest level, come down to racism and everything that comes with it, the reports that emerge from these organizations rarely acknowledge racism fully (structural and Whiteness). Rather, there is a half-hearted attempt to explain the reasons for such anomalies, with some trying to shift focus on societal or other factors. These other factors might intersect with race of course; however, institutional and structural racism is primary.

The usual accompanying sentence along the lines of, 'we have made progress, but there is more to do' is included in most reports and has done for a number of years. It is as if this sentence – appearing to be somewhat honest, open and vulnerable – will demonstrate the sincerity of commitment towards the race equality agenda. But for how long can organizations hide behind this. Ten years? Twenty? Fifty? At what point will those in powerful decision-making positions think that it is just not good enough and a different approach entirely is needed? The sentence 'we have made progress, but there is more to do' is similar to that of an alcoholic admitting to being an alcoholic, only really to obstruct people from pressing them to find the support they require, when in reality, they have no intention to stop drinking. These sorts of sentences are exhausted and appear to conceal the lack of work leading to tangible outcomes being carried out. Jackman and Muhe (1984) argue that White, educated people are willing to 'offer rhetorical support for equality but shy from doing anything to achieve it'[52] and I agree that is the case in most circumstances.

To illustrate my point on the seemingly open and vulnerable response to lack of progress that most organizations engage with, I turn to an open letter from writers Yasmin Abdel-Magied and Mariam Khan[53] about BBC Radio 4 *Woman's Hour* guest Zara Mohammed from the Muslim Council of Britain and her treatment on the show. Tim Davie, BBC Director-General stated this very sentiment in his response.

> …We have more work to do but we are determined to get there. Only last week we launched our staff diversity census, which will give our staff an opportunity to update their diversity data, including on religion. With this data we will have an up-to-date picture of staff diversity, which we can use to track staff retention, promotions and to identify areas of the organization which are under-represented and therefore need to work harder.[54]

The context is irrelevant really, although I shall briefly explain: Mohammed, the first woman to lead the Muslim Council of

Britain appeared on the BBC Radio 4 programme *Woman's Hour*. She was quizzed by the host, a White woman, and was repeatedly asked about female imams. Despite Mohammed stating that she did not have this information and it was beyond her role and remit, the host persisted with the questions. The show received numerous complaints and an open letter highlighting the lack of Muslim representation at the BBC. The letter was signed by over 100 people, including Afua Hirsch and Diane Abbott. Davie's response as above is typical of many that have gone before it in other contexts, the subtext of which is: we admit there is an issue ('cos we can't hide from the stats) and now, because we have been challenged, we have decided that this is important to us (it wasn't really before). I am being slightly facetious but you get the point.

The BBC interview took place on 4 February 2020, following which the BBC received many complaints – it may be cynical of me, but I have visions of senior leaders with their heads in their hands trying to conjure up some quick wins. Perhaps the census was a quick win that they could implement and use in their public communications? I feel, if this were viewed as important and necessary there may have been provisions already in place to make the changes required for an increase in Muslim representation. *Woman's Hour* would have briefed on how to handle that interview and the host would have been well versed in the tone that the BBC wanted to get across. Instead, what I feel we heard was bias and prejudice with hints of Islamophobia from the presenter. What Davie failed to acknowledge in his response was the undercurrent of racism. And as the many anecdotes and examples in this chapter show, this is symptomatic of a larger problem across many organizations and sectors in the UK.

To not see this as racism is a position of great privilege; to not want to acknowledge racism is also a position of privilege; to not speak up about racism and to be silent about its advantages is also privilege – afforded, in the main, to White people. This White solidarity, and silence as DiAngelo puts it, prevents progress; but most interesting to me is that I have observed Black and Brown people refrain from calling it out too. I am mortified to say that has also been me in the past. I have refrained from calling out covert racism in its many forms because I have feared it will prevent my progress professionally and it will impact how I am viewed. There have been occasions earlier on in my career where I have sat in meetings in a room full of senior people who are trying to explain away some racism and inequality that occurs in their line of work. I have rolled my eyes (internally) and wanted to state the reason loudly and clearly but have refrained because I know, as I did to code-switch, that this is not something Black and Brown people should do – for it shall end not so well. Most recently, the *Guardian* reported that the former cricketer Azeem Rafiq accused Yorkshire County Cricket Club of being institutionally racist receives abuse for speaking out.[55] I have seen this happen to others and most Black and Brown people I have spoken to also stated that only when they have reached a senior position might they feel comfortable – just might – to call it out. Even then, it has to be done ever so tactfully, and with much thought so as not to offend, agitate or alienate anyone or fracture the relationships that they have worked so hard to build.

I feel people and organizations flirt with the idea of race and racism but fail to commit and take the bullet to tackle it full on. Organizations sidestep around it, conjure up comfortable terms, and some Black and Brown people lose part of themselves to ensure that White people do not feel threatened or uncomfortable. However, this avoidance is a hindrance to progress and, as Eddo-Lodge states, 'seeing race is essential to changing the system.'[56]

It would be refreshing for those with power and influence to acknowledge that progress to date has been too slow and something quite radical is required for change. Equally, we need people (not just Black and Brown people) to call out institutional and structural racism, rather than to shy away from it for fear of repercussions and potential legal challenge.

To make progress on race equity and see positive outcomes for Black and Brown people we need to remove the façade and pretence displayed by some organizations that much work is taking place in this area. This might be true; however I refer to work that achieves tangible outcomes for Black and Brown people. I suggest that we should not waste our finite resources on long debates, discussions and research that do not talk about or address structural racism, Whiteness and power. We must remember that structures are created by people, and people can change these structures – these are constructs in themselves and not fixed entities.

And we need people (not just people of colour) to call out institutional and structural racism.

The reason George Floyd was murdered and other Black or Brown people continue to be treated abhorrently in my view, as I have stated previously, is structural and institutional racism. I don't think many sensible folks would argue that racism was a significant reason behind George Floyd's murder, but we also need to understand that White supremacy and the structural elements play their part. However, these more subtle and covert forms continue to go unchecked. The reason that the BBC presenter felt that she could ask those questions and be so forthright in her questioning was also structural racism and Whiteness; the reason there is underrepresentation at senior levels in mostly the largest organizations is also structural racism and Whiteness. Only when this is accepted and there is an honest and open acknowledgement (not a debate) can we start to break down and rebuild the structures in a fair and equitable manner. Only then will change occur. To be clear, I am not saying that racism and race are the only factors, but they are the most significant and they seem to be the only factors that are most likely to be debated.

Akala[57] argues that the idea of race is one of the most significant aspects of the modern world, having had a major impact on all areas of society and life. The general reticence towards discussing it 'reveals a palpable lack of interest in humanity'.[58]

There are some excellent resources available for organizations to support them in understanding the context of racism, where the gaps are and what can be done about it, some of which I mention on page 130.

Below I suggest some reflections to support good practice and provide an outline of what to avoid to help build organizations that genuinely want to embark on a journey to achieving race equity.

REFLECTIONS TO SUPPORT GOOD PRACTICE AND WHAT TO AVOID

- Have you provided learning on racism, institutional racism and structural racism? Talking about it will normalize conversations and building confidence through education, information and allies can support learning.
- Is your organization clear that this is not a critique of individual people but a system in which individuals engage, mostly unwittingly?
- Do you show honesty and integrity in the work you carry out to address inequality? – if you know your progress has been too slow, say so. Show your disappointment and commit to actions that will lead to tangible outcomes. Remember structures are created; therefore, there is an opportunity to change them.

Avoid

- Denying racism and structural racism exists, for example by citing a 'lack of evidence'. Evidence of institutional and structural racism cannot be found in individual and discrete cases: the evidence is in the disparities that we see in data.
- Are you bold and brave in addressing institutional and structural racism? Push boundaries, challenge bias and try

new things for example, shift the focus from supporting Black and Brown to climb the career ladder to addressing how senior leaders assess strengths and competencies and experience in recruitment.

- Feeling overwhelmed by the task of addressing racism; focus on one area at a time.

4

BROWN FEMINISM

Aseia Rafique

Introduction

There is not much out there which speaks to Brown feminists. But
we do exist. We have traditionally been excluded from mainstream
feminism, which hasn't spoken (and in my opinion, still doesn't
speak) to the experiences of Brown women. This might be because
there are many Brown voices, each speaking about what feminism
means to them, or it might just be a mismatch between religious
ideology and feminism – or a bit of both. A lot of it is not understanding the experiences and needs of Brown women, and this
is where bias inevitably rears its ugly head. There is also a lot of
criticism of White feminism's betrayal of Black and Brown women
and we are beginning to hear more and more documented about
the phenomenon known as 'White women's tears' (both inside
and outside the workplace) and the impact this has on Black and
Brown women. White women still experience privilege because
they are White, although they are still members of an oppressed
group because of their gender. And their tears can silence and
even demonize Black and Brown women. Why? Using tears in an
argument or a heated debate, or even being asked to take accountability for a racist remark or microaggression, means that some

White women portray themselves as the victim in such conflict situations, leading in many cases to White women crying and in tears. This then means a complete derailment of the actual argument or point being made by the Black or Brown woman, which in some instances has led to the Black and Brown being vilified for causing distress and making someone cry. As Ruby Hamad notes: 'When white women cry, it also makes them able to leave the conversation and choose not to listen.'[1]

The White kind of feminism

White women crying has become a powerful symbol of contradictions. On the one hand, it is seen as empathetic and in tune with struggles Black and Brown women face – crying is apologetic and of course, symbolic of wanting to do better and to offer support. But on the other hand, White women crying has also come to define the silencing of Brown and Black women. Crying shuts the conversation down and reframes White women as the victim; they are the ones that are hurting – after all? And the ensuing narrative is that if I (as a White woman), am here trying to support you as a Brown woman, but you are telling me I am part of the problem, then something is not quite right. As with the protests and conversations on anti-racism, the voices of Black and Brown women are getting louder – but breaking through the noise of recriminations and 'White' tears is not easy. I think it is difficult for some White women to see what their role might be or how they can help support Black and Brown women in the workplace. Although as women they face structural inequality and discrimination, they do not experience racism and may in fact be guilty of racism and racist attitudes themselves. It can be difficult to view yourself as an activist, fighting for women's rights, for example, and then having to acknowledge that, as a White woman, you may be part of the problem that reinforces White norms and values. The harm caused by decades of White women centring the conversation on themselves has meant that ultimately, messages of injustice and bias felt by Black and Brown women have gone unheard. Some White women are allies, want to help and want to understand, but some struggle to know what to do and how as an ally they can support others, either in everyday life or in the workplace. They could, for example in practical terms help review and put in place bias-free, inclusive organizational policies and processes, but so often I hear 'where do I start?' or 'what should I do first?' These questions and hesitations can alienate Black and Brown women, particularly if the White women in question hold senior positions. As a Brown woman I wonder how can it be so difficult. We can have a conversation, for example, and hear about some of the issues that Black and Brown people are experiencing and then work or support the organization to make the required changes. When gender and ethnicity pay gaps show Black women are paid less than White men and White women, then there is an issue that needs resolving. Black women are also the least likely to be among the UK's top earners compared to any other racial or gender group, according to a report published by the London School of Economics.

What can Black and Brown women do?

But should Black and Brown women tone down their stories and make them more palatable? Koa Beck in *White Feminism*[2] says, 'feminism has failed women of colour and that feminism may even be considered to be as oppressive as the patriarchy.' For some, there is a fury and defensiveness over being challenged about their lack of support for Brown and Black women. A noticeable sticking point is White women in management or leadership positions challenging attempts by Black and Brown women (who occupy fewer such positions) about their experiences of bias or racism. An example of this is inviting and holding conversations with Black and Brown women about their workplace experiences and then ignoring (or doing nothing) about what has been shared. Other microaggressions, such as moving on quickly when Black and Brown women contribute in a meeting discussion are left for Black and Brown women to resolve. Even identifying the actions that can be taken to help remove such microaggressions but not taking the lead to support colleagues to deliver on this is another example of closing the conversation down on racist practices. Other examples I have seen is allowing junior colleagues to carry out research on discrimination and then actively ignoring the findings. I have seen and heard senior White women visibly sigh or put their hands over their faces in meetings when racism or equality, diversity and inclusion are discussed. And there are many times when senior leaders simply do not attend such meetings at all. It is the 'not doing anything' that is an issue. A recently observed trend is to discuss anti-racism, bias or inclusion in theoretical terms, such as conceptually looking at 'problems' through a 'theory of change' or the 'paradoxical theory of change'. Such discussions are not unhelpful, but when they do not translate into actions and theories are discussed with increasing regularity at every meeting, the perception I am being given is that such discussions are a way to derail, slow down or stop the more practical conversation on race and racism.

Where has that support been? It is difficult to forget that minority voices were left out of the suffragettes' movement and that the movement itself was shaded by racism and White supremacy. At its peak, it was, of course, operating in the context of the British Empire, and inevitably imperialist views infiltrated its ranks. The achievement of women finally getting the vote in 1928, with women in England, Wales and Scotland receiving the vote on the same terms as men, benefitted White women over Black and Brown women, many of whom were still serving as domestic helpers in the homes of White suffragettes. Many White women insist they cannot be part of the problem; they are too nice and simply not built that way, but, when issues of race and racism and bias crop up, the institutional focus settles on the struggles of White women and still fails to address distinct forms of oppression faced by Black and Brown women. The marginalization of Black and Brown women in White feminist spaces is well documented, as Kimberlé Crenshaw notes in her critique, *The Intersection of Race and Sex: A Black Feminist Critique of Antidiscrimination Doctrine, Feminist Theory and Antiracist Politics.*[3] This marginalization is structural and systemic, and existing within it is the gatekeeping of White spaces, fields of knowledge and entry into positions of power.

Some White women happily exclude themselves from the conversation and I have seen many examples of this. I have received emails questioning 'why there is so much focus on equality, diversity and inclusion', or I have been told 'our organization' has 'diversity fatigue'! I have heard many times at work that we should leave taking action on anti-racism and inclusivity to a proposed date in the future because there is so much 'other' (more important) work that needs to be completed first. Perhaps there is a reluctance to offer opinions on race or discrimination because it might take away the platform from Black and Brown people who, because of Black Lives Matter, have felt able to highlight (sometimes for the very first time) some of their issues and concerns. But excusing yourself from the conversation simply means being a passive recipient of information on injustice and exclusion. Offering insight and opinions helps to frame bias and can be an opportunity to discuss solutions. It is never good enough to remain silent or use silence as an option to remove yourself from the conversation. It is not helpful to people who experience bias to have to sort it out. And challenging intersectional bias, for example, the lack of Black and Brown women in senior leadership positions, isn't something I have personally heard White women advocate for. Sharing articles, information and discussions on anti-racism, microaggressions and other forms of prejudice on social media, is more often than not an activity supported and 'liked' by other Black and Brown women. I have been in discussions with White women who have said they are interrogating themselves about bias and about power and White privilege and White supremacy. What that means and how it may manifest itself, is a helpful first step, but sometimes it feels like the conversation and personal introspection about racism and White privilege is holding back some White women who are perhaps keen to take action. I'm not sure. Some Black and Brown people don't want to wait until White people or White women are ready to support us.

Much as we talk about feminism and the rights we should afford to those that are particularly vulnerable (for example, victims of honour killings, unjust imprisonment and the like), the feminism that has come to dominate society and media is White, Western feminism. It is the kind of feminism that excludes other identities; it is the kind where White men and women continue to force their views on others and where we endlessly debate the whys and wherefores of the exclusion of Brown and Black women in popular culture by celebrities such as Lena Dunham and Amy Schumer.

We rarely hear about feminism from Brown women and, if we do, such struggles rarely make it into the mainstream White conscious. 'Reclaim the Night', a protest fighting for the rights of women to be able to go out at night without fear of violence and murder, marching in 'pussy hats' and other actions taken by women to fight for equality, rights and justice are hugely important, but imagine trying to explain to a Brown family why you are wearing a 'pussy hat' or why you are going out at night – a lot of young Brown women are not even allowed out at this time! I know, because I was one of those who wasn't!

We are *not* in this together. History tells us that those fighting for women's rights have been White and wealthy enough to have had the time and resources to fight inequality and injustice. I personally felt the lack of a feminist support system for Brown women growing up, and my mother could have done with some feminism back then – she was nineteen years old when she joined my father in her new home in the heart of the Black Country, as mentioned earlier. Then and today, the Black Country is home to some of the most economically deprived areas in Britain. And from the moment she arrived, her choices dwindled, her movements were restricted. She was young, Brown and female and, unfortunately for her, feminism was nowhere to be seen. But these were the 1960s and 1970s when second-wave feminism was sweeping through the UK and bringing with it some changes and equality for women. The 1960s, for example, brought the contraceptive pill and a sexual revolution and the majority of White women were motivated, rightly so, to try to abolish sexism and highlight the sexist attitudes they experienced at work and at home. The year 1968 saw the Dagenham strike for equal pay for women and the *Feminine Mystique* by Betty Friedan was published in 1963. For feminism this was an iconic time, but for Brown women, and in particular for Brown women like my mum, first entering the UK, these two worlds remained wholly apart, and I don't even think they have managed to merge, even today. The pill was not something I was told about (sex before marriage was strictly forbidden), apart from the fact that it could help with acne, explained to me by a Doctor once. Many of the Brown families I knew had four or more children. As for a sexual revolution – highly laughable and never, ever mentioned. Oh my goodness, can you imagine, discussing sex for women in highly conservative Brown families?! The pressure to be a 'good wife' for Brown women remains stubbornly intact, with expectations of moving into a husband's home after marriage, being able to cook well and showing that you are an excellent host at large gatherings, as well as having an intact hymen, still much-coveted.

What was happening instead was that Brown women joining partners from abroad, having recently been married or waiting to be married – or otherwise, were being checked at the airport by immigration officers to make sure they were virginally intact.[4] Virginity tests, a new low, reflected the prejudices still in place in the 1960s and 70s. Immigration rules at the time meant that a woman coming into the UK to marry did not need a visa if her wedding was to be held within three months. But virginity tests took place where there were 'suspicions' that women may already be married, meaning they needed a visa, or were deemed to be 'too old' to be a bride. An article from the *Guardian* in 2011 suggests that at least '80 female migrants from the subcontinent may have undergone such tests at the time.'[5] These tests, given mainly to South Asian women seeking to enter the UK on fiancé visas, were performed because officials believed they were entering Britain under false pretences. Pratihba Parmar, author of the chapter 'Gender, Race and Class: Asian Women in Resistance' in *The Empire Strikes Back: Race and Racism in 70s Britain*, by Marmo and Smith, believed 'that the racist and sexist assumptions behind "virginity testing"' were based on the 'stereotype of the submissive, meek and tradition-bound Asian woman',[6] a stereotype which continues today.

Black women are also stereotyped, but in contrast to South Asian women, they are consistently stereotyped as aggressive and overtly sexual. These can be difficult stereotypes to break out of and sadly, often accepted as fact by others. On a university exchange trip to Braunschweig in Germany, I was looked after by a wonderful family who wanted to loan me the use of a bike so I could get around the city with ease. I didn't take up the offer straight away as I was getting used to my new surroundings and just really trying to orientate myself. A couple of weeks in, I asked if I could borrow the bike and because I hadn't jumped at the offer straight away, they had assumed that being a Brown woman, I hadn't taken up the offer because I had not learned or had been prevented from learning how to ride a bike.

And in an interview once, when describing my skills in answer to some question, the feedback I was given was that I had been 'too confident and self-assured' in the depiction of my skills. And no, I didn't get the job! I have experienced countless micro-aggressions over the years which gave me the message that I was either not good enough or too assertive for 'what was expected' of a Brown woman. Strategies, I have come to realize, that are more about trying to keep Brown women in their place and trying to reduce the space they inhabit than trying to encourage and empower Black and Brown women in the workplace. Why else are Brown women mistaken for one another, even when they look nothing alike? I understand that it is easy to forget names or genuinely mistake people for others who may look or dress similarly, but persistently mistaking people for others quickly becomes wilful ignorance. I have heard of instances where two Brown women from different continents and with different hair colours have been mistaken for each other. I wonder why it is that Black and Brown people get regularly mistaken for one another. Our brains help us to consolidate and process information quickly and similar physical characteristics, such as the colour of people's skin, may be one way our brain is helping us to make such decisions. This can be done innocently enough, but on deeper probing, it is often the result of a laziness on the part of White people who are of the opinion (even subconsciously) that 'all Black and Brown people look the same'. The laziness actually derives from racism; for example, Marcus Rashford, a prominent footballer and activist was mistaken for England and Saracens rugby star Maro Itoje by Education Secretary Gavin Williamson, and the comedian Nish Kumar has been referred to as Nish Patel and been mistaken for Ahir Shah, a fellow Asian comedian. Kumar has frustratingly said that 'when it's an institution that gets money from me. When you make money off my name, you learn my damn name.'[7]

This 'phenomenon' of looking the same as another person with brown skin stretches back as far as I can remember and has even become a conversation starter, when speaking to other fellow Brown women. Even lawyers are not immune, with one colleague explaining they regularly received emails for another 'Priya' in the firm, and even calling it out didn't make it stop.

Muslim feminists exist

This 'helplessness' of the Brown woman extends into religious doctrine, and nowhere more so than for the Muslim woman. Being a Brown feminist can be a balancing act in and of itself, but being a Muslim feminist is something else altogether – in particular, if personal beliefs come into conflict with cultural and religious expectations. I know this, having seen it first-hand. It wasn't that long ago, and even as late as the 1970s, when women were being refused mortgages and still needed the signature of a male guarantor to be able to buy a house; and if they tried to buy a drink in a pub before 1982, it was legal to refuse to serve a woman. 'Really – 1982?' I hear you say. 'That isn't that long ago.' True, but buying a drink and especially buying alcohol in a pub wasn't something the Brown women I knew aspired to do. Owning property, yes, but buying a drink in a pub, well, not really. I remember a domestic violence issue involving a young Brown woman recently married from overseas and going with my father to the local pub where she had decided to wait for us to see if we could help. My father told me to wait by the roadside kerb way away from the pub just in case I was tainted by its very presence.

So feminism was not a word I associated with Brown women. I didn't see it in action and rarely saw or heard from Brown women in the media. I watched Meera Syal in *Goodness Gracious Me* and even now, decades later, she is still one of the biggest Brown women stars I know. Unfortunately, I seldom come across a confident, powerful, purposeful Brown woman on TV and in the media. And feminism is definitely not a word associated with Brown Muslim women. In fact, feminism has come to be seen as the antithesis of what a Muslim woman represents. 'Seriously, how can you be Brown, female, feminist *and* a Muslim?' are the whispers I hear in people's minds. Representation of Muslim women in the media generally depicts them in a pejorative way and rarely provides a voice to these women or their achievements. And I have had conversations with colleagues who believe that these two things, Muslim and feminist, are contradictory and unable to co-exist. What I have understood by these conversations is that if Muslim women *were* empowered, then why are they dressed in 'prohibitive' clothing and in some cases acquiesce and agree with cultural practices, such as using separate prayer facilities, that show their subservience to men?

As poet Suhaiymah Manzoor-Khan on the BBC Radio 4 podcast series *How to Be a Muslim Woman*[8] said, 'I am simply not allowed to be a Muslim and a feminist.' There are more female Muslim voices articulating that we need to change the way we talk about Muslim women, highlighting that we need to show the details and nuances of Brown women's lives in the same way we do for White women.

And there is not a conversation that goes by about Muslim women that does not mention clothing. The strength of feeling and the laws that are passed are themselves quite curious. France became the first European country to ban the full-face Islamic veil in public places in 2011 and in 2020 confirmed that its years-long ban on wearing burqas, niqabs and other full-face coverings in public would remain in place. Swimming in a burkini often makes headlines and elicits negative responses from those reporting on it,[9] and of course we have Boris Johnson with his commentary that the niqab looks like a 'letterbox'.[10] The *Independent* quoted that Islamophobic incidents rose by 375 per cent after Johnson made this remark. In a Facebook post on face coverings advocating for women to have autonomy over what they wear and when, the responses received were completely predictable:

'How about Muslims walk away from Islam instead?'

'Why would a woman choose to wear a hijab – because she wants to show everyone that she believes in a religion which persecutes women?'

But why the fascination with what someone else is wearing? If a woman chooses to wear a burqa, niqab or anything else, why is that a problem for someone else? White feminism has long tried to shake the perception that the clothes women wear, whether that is a short skirt, low top or nothing at all – is a woman's choice and clothing should neither be the focal point nor blamed for the abuse or violence women across the world experience. But where are the voices of White women advocating for the right of Muslim women to wear what they want? I find it painful that the condemnation and disapproval about what Muslim women wear is so great – and fail to understand why this creates such a furore. The nature of the clothes and 'covering up' must, I believe, feed into the subversiveness of what is 'deemed acceptable' in White Western society and clearly wearing a burqa isn't the right fit for how Western civilization wants to see itself, pretending instead that we are living in liberal progressive societies.

And of course, the paradox is that there *is* injustice for many women over what they wear. Not all women are able to choose, either because of misplaced paternalism, oppression or internalized patriarchy. Women, and from my experience many Brown women, are socialized to believe that patriarchy works for all of us, and it takes conscious effort on a personal and political level to counteract what many of us have normalized as the right kind of acceptable behaviour. For example, I have argued many times about why it is that women and girls are the ones that are pushed to learn how to cook, clean and 'look after' men and boys. This, in my family, has been countered by lectures about 'acceptable' female behaviour. I have been told I shouldn't go running, that I shouldn't go to the gym or even to evening college lectures as I should be at home looking after my husband. I have been told stories about 'good' daughters-in-law and 'bad' ones, but I have never been told similar stories about sons-in-law. I have even been told that times have changed for the worse and these days there are too many Brown women who are proud, over-educated and arrogant, especially when they turn down marriage proposals. I want feminism to support Black and Brown women in changing behaviour, reducing the inequality women face and 'dismantling the patriarchy', a term which means to 'seek freedom from patriarchy and all forms of oppression that exploit and devalue women',[11] but feminism is something I have engaged with, with other Brown women and never with White and Brown women together. I think this is because there is little interest from some White women in discrimination which specifically relates to Black and Brown women.

When the word feminist is mentioned, I have also seen Brown people become uncomfortable and change the subject. It is particularly difficult when I know of Brown women who are married to much older men, some as old as their father and even grandfather. The women I know have come from abroad and how much this was a choice or how much this was enforced by others is difficult to know as nobody wants to discuss or talk about this. But where is the support of feminism to help Black and Brown women mobilize against the bias and discrimination they experience at home and in the workplace? More female White allies are needed.

And so although White modern feminism centres patriarchy as a concept through which to understand the different ways gendered oppression can be understood, it still does not support minority women to dismantle the systems in which they have been caught.

White feminism does not discuss or stray into religion or belief. It can be difficult, I know, but if women voiced some of the issues they were facing together with White and Black and Brown voices, there might be more understanding of the issues and nuances around the everyday lived experience of some Black and Brown women. For example, over the years I have been asked why Muslim women are not allowed to pray or fast when we are on our period. I don't really have an answer to this, but grew up believing that having a period was 'unclean'. Why else wasn't I allowed to pray or fast at this time? Questioning several aunts about this, I was told that giving women a break from fasting when they are feeling down or suffering from back pain or experiencing mood swings helped women – so all in all a considerate thing to do. I believe this is misplaced paternalism and internalized misogyny. Such an answer does not extend to asking women whether they wanted or needed a break. There are thousands of women very healthily and happily going about their daily lives while also having a period. But talking about religion in general or questioning the tenets of religion or belief to family, friends or colleagues who believe in that faith is tantamount to blasphemy, and even discussing such 'sensitive things' or hard-hitting topics, such as the fact that we need to work harder to eradicate female genital mutilation, for example, brings anger and fury from those who want to continue to hold power over other Black and Brown women. This power, in my opinion, is held by men and upheld by some women, including some White women. But highlighting such injustices can improve women's lives. Why is it that Black and Brown women are expected to get involved in women's rights, in feminism, but only when the topics being advocated for, for example sexual harassment in the workplace, are being viewed through a White lens? I learned about sexual harassment of Black and Brown colleagues not through any conversations I had with White women but conversations I had with Black and Brown women.

The conflict of covering up

Choice is a tricky business and nowhere more so than in the clothes you wear – and how much – or how little you decide to 'cover up'. Covering up as a Brown woman is political – too much and you are branded as a fundamentalist or 'oppressed', too little and you've become 'Westernized', 'modern' and not the right kind of Brown woman others (that is, some Brown men and White women) are looking for. Such conflicts can literally wear (no pun intended) you down, and trying to realize others' expectations of the clothes that can or cannot be worn is overbearing and simply exhausting. From White women in particular, I have received many comments on my clothing choices over the years (disclaimer: some of the comments concerned clothes that I wore back in the 1990s, so not great fashion choices, I must admit), such as, 'That's a lovely ethnic jumper you have on' (it was a jumper from Marks & Spencer); 'It's nice to see a young girl covering up' (this one for wearing a long-sleeved top); or, 'Aren't you too hot?' for not wearing a t-shirt in hot weather. And similarly, having been policed by White people, Brown people are also judging. From a Brown Muslim woman, I once had: 'Your kameez is see-through – can you go home and change?' and: 'You can't wear a sleeveless dress – your brothers won't like it.' This policing of Brown women's bodies is constant, with bias and judgement running across cultures. One, it is annoying, and two, it is no one else's business what Brown women, or any woman, wears. It is a shame this happens though, and for me, I have had many an internal battle and been in constant flux of having to think about the 'right' kind of clothes to wear. Some of my Brown female friends have had similar issues, with some even refusing to wear traditional Asian dress to go to work, go shopping or anywhere that was felt to be a non-Asian space. I have even, I am ashamed to admit it, changed clothes to go to work in, in order to work in peace. Fighting for your rights is never as easy as it sounds! But I do believe that if we had solidarity from White feminists in our quest to help change the narrative of wearing what we wished, at work and outside of work, then more Brown women would feel comfortable in their clothing choices and help increase the diversity of 'White' spaces.

The one piece of clothing, however, which never fails to cause collective hysterical paroxysm and interestingly enough which also has maximum visibility, is the headscarf. Because it is linked to faith and because some Muslim scholars believe it is obligatory in Islamic law for women to wear the hijab, the question of the hijab (or the veil) is one of the most controversial issues to take hold in both Muslim and non-Muslim countries. It is inextricably tied up with faith, freedom and women's bodies and has been reduced to conversations about how and why women should be covered, to the 'right' colour, thickness and uniformity of a headscarf. For me, the struggle has been with the wearing – or not wearing – of a headscarf or dupatta, a piece of clothing which conventionally forms a 'ghoonghat' or veil from the outside world.

Yes, the headscarf *is* political, causes paroxysms of outrage in many non-wearers, and, as researchers and academics have voiced before me, it is where the personal becomes the political and vice versa. Wearing a headscarf is a political statement. Being a Black or Brown woman is a political statement. The headscarf, whether it is a beautifully embroidered piece of material or a plain, single-coloured scarf, is a battleground playing out between moral, religious and gender rights and 'normative' behaviour. The headscarf may seem benign on the surface but has fast become a symbol of cultural and religious division – between societies and between the sexes – in politics and even as a direct power struggle with patriarchy. In 2019, for example, a social media campaign of Iranian women taking photos of themselves without headscarves meant that such 'transgressors' could face a ten-year prison sentence. An even more daring backlash occurred when husbands put on the burka and a headscarf in solidarity and support of their wives to show the oppressive nature and discomfort in wearing these items. This campaign and others continue to grow and even as they grow, there are others looking to suppress and keep women in their place.

Having never continuously worn a dupatta, I have, nevertheless, collected many of them over the years. They lie neatly folded away in small, square, colourful piles in my drawers and suitcases (Brown women always have suitcases full of elaborate clothes – many of which are stored on top of wardrobes). The dupatta, as opposed to the close-fitted headscarf usually associated with Muslim women's attire, is a long floaty piece of material that comes together with, and is part of, the traditional Punjabi outfit of a salwar and a kameez. For me, growing up, this was a necessary but tiresome piece of clothing. This beautiful piece of raw silk or cotton or fine gossamer, or whatever material that happened to come together in the same pattern as the salwar and kameez, was an outfit that had to be worn when visiting other Brown families. We always had to wear one as a mark of respect in front of elders, at a place of worship, and while reciting prayers. I often obsessed over it – how should I wear it? – off the shoulder, around the neck or tied around the waist if I was to be very daring. You could loop it into a V shape perhaps or over your shoulders or, if you wanted to, you could drape or tie the scarf on your head. I was forever anxious about how much needed to be draped in front of me for modesty purposes – or would it be OK if I just let it rest simply around my neck? I liked that look and it was easy to wear, but the continuing question in my head was whether it would be too rebellious, even frowned upon.

Should I simply cover up like most of the Brown women I saw? For this reason, I never really committed to wearing a dupatta when I didn't have to. It just got in the way. I tripped over it; my mind tripped over it. I saw some women wearing it effortlessly and I felt guilty. I felt more White and less Brown. I saw how beautiful it could look and that made me stress and worry about why I couldn't carry off such a look. I rarely wore a dupatta on my head. The material was too smooth and slippery to stay in place and I was too lazy to pin it on. And besides, it wasn't expected of me that I had to do that, and I felt glad I didn't have to. I could not move away from the association of 'covering up' with that of having to be submissive to others, and in particular, submissive to men.

I always felt a bit guilty and a bit grateful that I did not have to wear a headscarf or carry a dupatta around with me (when not visiting other Asian households). At school, there were many girls whose families adapted the school uniform so their children could wear a Salwar and Kameez in the navy blue school colours, with a navy-blue dupatta. A visible underclass of pupils whose first-generation parents were consciously and constantly alarmed at the freedom of expression and clothing they saw White girls displaying. Although I love the look and feel of a dupatta, I found it impractical and annoying to wear every day. And I felt most annoyed at the way women and girls had to have coverage, whereas boys and men were free to wear what pleased them. As Nikesh Shukla said in his book *Brown Baby, A Memoir of Race, Family and Home*, 'societal norms pervade in ways we cannot always see.'[12] I wanted to fit in, but at the same time disliked the connotations and the perception that I was seen as 'vulnerable' and 'less than a man'.

You cannot get a more feminine item of clothing, or any apparel more politically fraught, than the headscarf. But nobody should be forced to wear something they do not want to, and there are many arguments that girls do not have to wear one – although I still see instances of children in a headscarf. I have heard Black and Brown women say that the more the headscarf is frowned upon, and the more negative associations White society attaches to it, the more they want to wear one, reclaim it and shout about it. They want to tie it closer, make sure it fits better, make sure they stand out in the world – for wearing a scarf – and that this is who they choose to be. To my knowledge, the headscarf is not something that is discussed by White feminists, or advocated for by them on behalf of Black and Brown women who wear it. I know for some White feminists it is seen as a form of oppression that exploits and devalues women, but to have a radical transformation about the way women in headscarves are perceived, White women need to be part of this conversation to change attitudes on racism. It is a huge burden to challenge power structures and socially constructed norms and, as I mentioned earlier, we need White women allies to support Black and Brown women to do this.

The headscarf has reverence for some of the Brown, Black and, occasionally, the White women who wear it. However, it is still looked at with aversion by others. I find it is often the elephant in the room. No matter how lovely, the headscarf has come to symbolize the oppression and subjugation of women. The same point is never made for Sikh men wearing the turban – they have patriarchy on their side, and coercion has never come into it. But no matter how often people may praise the beauty of a headscarf, I always note the look in others' eyes when they first come face to face with a scarf-wearer. The headscarf cannot be criticized or discussed without enflaming opinions. When faith is involved, we have learned that silence is sometimes the only option, presenting its own challenges, disallowing debate and discussion and refuting real choice. Paradoxically, the headscarf (the veil) is also a symbol of romance: the soft fabric of the dupatta that is venerated in Bollywood films, romantically, billowing gently – and coyly – in the breeze, as a symbol of captive femininity, modesty and female sexuality.

The headscarf, with all of its complexities, has risen to become a symbol of diversity. No work publication or staff newsletter is ready to go out into the world without a picture of a woman in a headscarf in it. As the face of diversity at her organization, one woman told me she was constantly asked by her workplace if they could use her image on marketing materials. It didn't seem to matter if she worked in the team that wanted to use her photo or whether she had anything to do with the service or product being marketed. The headscarf has become the new tick box, whether frowned upon or accepted. As we already know, however, a Black or Brown woman – or a woman of colour in a headscarf – is the person least likely to be heading up an organization as CEO or managing director, but one of the most likely to be 'the face of diversity'.

Brown women are at once invisible and visible, in purdah or out of purdah. I find it slightly ironic that the pre-election period in the UK, sometimes known as 'purdah', describes the period of time immediately before elections or referendums, when specific restrictions on communications activity are in place. The use of this term parallels the restrictions faced by women in purdah and enforced by men. They are expected to be passive, homemakers and silent. This stereotype has made it difficult for some Brown women to find their voice in the workplace. And when they do, they are up against perceptions of the 'right' way to behave from both within their own community and from outside of it.

Fighting for feminism

Tellingly, feminism has become a successful global export, popular in society, culture and the media. Beyoncé owned the word in her 2014 VMA performance and later the #MeToo movement took predatory men and society to task. In late 2018, #MainBhi, Pakistan's very own 'Me Too' was pushed to the fore after the rape and murder of seven-year-old Zainab Ansari in January 2018. And while Pakistani activist Malala continues her fight for girls' education, feminism continues to highlight global injustice. We can feel both the presence of feminism and resistance to it, right across the world. But we need more feminism for Brown women and a push back against internalized patriarchal norms, which, unfortunately, many Brown women themselves have internalized and continue to perpetuate.

The realities, struggles and vulnerabilities of Brown women are all around us. Yet it is the story of the Brown woman who looks you straight in the eye, tells you that she has rejected all notions of having an arranged marriage and that she has successfully rebelled against her own parents by 'running away from home' or has just moved out to begin her journey as an independent woman that people want to hear. They pay attention to the mischievous, twinkly eyed Brown woman sticking two fingers up to the world telling everyone 'she has "escaped"' – and now happily and conveniently fits perfectly into the White Western narrative of the 'right kind', the 'only kind' of Brown feminism others want to see.

But of course, it is possible to be a feminist without rejecting your history or cultural background. Finding the balance between culture, religion, tradition and feminism lies in understanding that these aren't mutually exclusive. There is no 'right', 'wrong' or 'bad' feminism. But what is it that Brown feminists are up against?

It's not just the traditional notion of having to fight against 'the patriarchy' but also juggling for space in their own culture, and their own communities. The lives of Brown women are trapped in a cycle of religious and cultural purity, femininity, beauty *and* complicity. Brown women, marginalized from White feminist progress, are also silent and complicit in perpetuating abuse and violence against other Brown women. In India, for example and other countries, simply not wanting a girl has led to a serious skewing of the birth rate in favour of boys. The underlying cause of abandonment and female infanticide is deep-rooted and continues to strangle and kill women who are born Brown.

This is about the double and triple jeopardy that many Brown women face. Visible as the caregiver in the home and maybe as a matriarch in the community, she is still dismissed as being less than a man and being less than a White woman.

Sometimes you have to break cultural expectations and learn to be proud of your culture without having to sacrifice who you are. There are Brown women out there looking to change and challenge the status quo. For example, the Pink Ladoo[13] campaign highlights the injustice of celebrating a boy's birth over a girl's. The fight back has begun and rightly so. The re-education and misinformation aimed at Brown women is also a work in progress.

The fight of Brown women has different challenges, and these are challenges and barriers that White women have struggled to comprehend. History is stacked against the Brown woman, the minority, the other. She is easy to silence, and for some has been forced to conform to religious and cultural stereotypes and continue a tradition where women are seen as the nurturer and men as the provider. And, as is so often the case, to belong, to be part of something that is bigger than themselves, many Brown women accept their role, take a back seat and suppress their ambitions.

Such belonging to an 'in group', is desirable however; it is a space where other Brown women come together, where you can participate in the language, and seamlessly fit into the codes of that group. It is part of your identity. This wish to belong is reinforced by ties of friendship and family. If this is right for other Brown women, then it must be right for you. Whenever I step back into that world, I feel a mix of emotions, of seeing what might have been. I breathe in my childhood again and breathe out the adult I am now. The familiarity is overwhelming. But when visiting a recently bereaved close family friend to offer my condolences one day, I walked into a world of binary oppositions – women in one house, men in another. Women speaking quietly and praying, men standing outside chatting.

This means that in times of celebration or mourning, in many South Asian cultures, women are separated from the men. I cannot now remember the number of weddings I attended as a small child, where a wedding hall was quite literally split into half. Sometimes, it would be huge screens that broke up the room but more often than not there were side rooms where families were separated by sex. Having to eat and drink and celebrate, not with your own family but only with half of them, always left me wondering. The backdrop to such separation left me feeling slightly suspicious, and wondering why families could not simply sit together.

And then, when the occasion and attitudes allowed, I would suddenly go from women-only spaces to a mixed hall of guests. Why the difference? The Brown woman, in my experience, has to navigate this world, mould herself to the expectations placed on her to whatever the occasion demanded.

I think what mattered to me was the inequality of it all. Why were Brown women considered as less by everyone around them? Even today, when I read about what Brown people have been up to, how they have celebrated a religious festival or a family wedding, it is always the women who explain what they have cooked, decided to wear and even whom to visit. I was not even surprised when reading a 'day in the life' – a corporate fixture of the working world and an effort to personalize and make 'the office' environment more human – of someone who contributed their story about the celebration of Eid. What saddened me was that the person described the family waking up, the women going into the kitchen to prepare breakfast and then again to prepare dinner and how lovely it was. There was not a hint of irony, just accepted fact, and the normalization of 'this is how it works'. But where do those of us go who want something different?

And in deeply conservative and religious countries such as Pakistan, men still hold power and sway in the most personal parts of women's lives. On a trip to Pakistan, I was taken aback and surprised that bras were sold by men to women. Men owned and ran businesses, including the selling of women's clothes and underwear. If you needed a new bra, the shop owner, a man, would look at you to see the size he felt you needed and sell you a bra. There was no chance to try it on to see if it fit and you had to take what you got. Fantastical, unnerving and simply wrong!

REFLECTIONS ON GOOD PRACTICE

- Do think about Brown and Black women when thinking about rights for women.
- Speak with Black and Brown women and listen to their stories.
- Talk about and discuss Black and Brown women's stories with White women.
- Use your activism to highlight the inequality and concerns facing Black and Brown women as well as White women.
- Look at feminism from a Black and Brown perspective as a well as through a White lens.
- When thinking about dismantling and changing the way patriarchy works, think about how patriarchy also manifests itself for Black and Brown women.
- Encourage Black and Brown women to join protest movements.

Avoid

- Don't silence Black and Brown women by ignoring the issues that concern them.
- Don't silence Black and Brown women's stories by centring the issue on yourself.
- Don't think feminism doesn't matter to Black and Brown women.
- Attend events hosted by women of colour to understand concerns and issues.
- Take the time to make sure you do not confuse Brown and Black women with one another.
- Don't pre-judge Black and Brown women because of cultural traditions.
- Don't say, 'I don't see colour.'

5

THE FUTURE – TRANSFORMATIONAL OR TRANSACTIONAL?

Vanisha Parmar

We have discussed some of the reasons why racial equity has not yet been achieved. So, what now – is there any light at the end of tunnel? Firstly, we have to accept what has been done to date has not proved too successful if we consider the copious amounts of data that are published nationally on all areas in society, or if we consider data and information on a micro-organizational level. There may have been some small success as a result of some initiative or another but reports such as 'The Colour of Power'[1] demonstrate that our progress is too slow. While this chapter is in the main organization-focused and comes together from the experience of working in different sectors with many people at all levels and positions on the spectrum of allyship – some of the principles I lay out can be applied in a societal and social context.

Less transactional and more transformational

Can race equity ever be achieved? Yes indeed, but it requires some real changes to make it happen; we can't continue with the same actions and initiatives; the evidence suggests they simply don't work.

A transformational approach to tackling racial inequality is the single biggest thing that an organization can do to achieve racial equity. A transformational approach requires addressing racial inequality at an institutional and structural level. This approach requires work to address racism by dismantling the way in which organizations are structured and built with focus on equitable outcomes that will achieve racial equity. What does this mean? It means that organizations have to manoeuvre themselves out of their comfort zones and put the work in, but it can be done if there is a genuine desire and a level of honesty. A transactional approach, in contrast, focuses on individual interventions centred around attempts to change behaviours and outcomes for individuals. This approach is one that most large organizations currently take and have been taking for some time, and while it may result in some very small changes it is limited in the attainment of racial equity.

I feel there is a strong belief amongst many organizations that there has been a significant change in how race is being progressed since George Floyd's murder. I often hear phrases like, 'We've seen a massive culture shift'; 'Race is really on the agenda' and/or 'We are having open and frank conversations'. While I agree to some degree about the 'culture shift', this has been momentary for some organizations. As I mentioned previously, the dust seems to have settled. For me, this culture shift and partaking in discussions about race does not go far enough to make progress. Rather, it seems to nestle in a cuddly blanket – it's comfortable and cosy.

Transformational practice is anti-racist practice; it is a practice that makes changes to policy, or intentionally creates policy with the aim of ensuring racial equity by moving away from the traditional equality approach. This sort of approach requires committed and engaged leadership and middle managers that supports the idea that Black and Brown people are not the problem; Black and Brown people do need more training and support; that Black and Brown people are neither lacking nor have something wrong with them; that Black and Brown people are educated enough; that Black and Brown people do not hold themselves back – but rather, it is the policies that exist that hold Black and Brown people back from achieving. It is not talent that Black and Brown people lack; it is the whiteness they lack. It is not that Black and Brown people are more deviant; it is that they are seen as such for not conforming to the boundaries set by white structures. It is not that they are less adept at following regulations or sticking to regulatory boundaries of compliance; it is that the measures based around these are skewed towards a standard of whiteness.

A good example of where changes can be made is making sure recruitment pipelines are anti-racist: this means changing practices and processes surrounding recruitment to achieve an outcome of racial equity and avoiding racial homogeneity. It can include:

- breaking the practice of obtaining candidates only from certain schools, colleges and universities and existing networks that have limited diversity;

- removing the requirement of certain educational levels such as degrees;

- training your hiring managers and panellist in anti-racism;

- ensuring an objective, equality-proofed set of criteria that focus on talent rather than experience;

- setting realistic and challenging targets; and

- hiring managers insisting on diverse shortlists.

Another example might be shifting the focus from career workshops for Black and Brown people to career workshops for hiring managers that focus on changing structures to permit more Black and Brown people through the system. For many organizations, policies and practices remain the same – there is lack of scrutiny or an unwillingness to radically alter the structures. I find that more resources are plugged into well intentioned, discrete interventions that may or may not result in a positive outcome for a few individuals. These transactional approaches are limited. If Black and Brown people are not applying, being interviewed for, and successfully appointed to positions or places in educational settings, and if appointed/accepted not continuing to stay in those institutions, it is probably very likely due to the policies, processes, culture and people. If organizations and institutions genuinely want Black and Brown people, who bring with them a level of authenticity and confidence to be themselves they can make it happen. How? By removing all the unnecessary barriers that prevent them in the first place. Senior leaders, managers and teams have the power to make this happen (if they want it to). This is not about positively discriminating – it is about removing barriers and hurdles. This isn't about 'letting people off', giving more to one group over another unfairly or lowering the bar, but it is about creating a system to achieve fair outcomes. Perhaps traditionally there has been far too much focus on creating a process that is equal to everyone; but we must bear in mind that this approach is based on the assumption that everyone is at the same level of chance and opportunity and there is true meritocracy – there isn't. This is just not true.

Transformational work is an ongoing process – it is not a one-off project – and is very necessary if we want to see a shift. A change to the way we approach what we do, such as recruitment as I mentioned, how we measure competence, how we set up our criteria, how we interview, who interviews, will be for the benefit of everyone, not just certain groups. This approach can be adopted and adapted no matter what the function – education, employment, regulation, justice – whatever.

Transformational work might seem daunting; however, this is not something that can be achieved in a short time and then ticked off as complete. A good place to start is an objective and brutally honest analysis of where an organization currently is, followed by a prioritization action plan based on the biggest gaps and concerns. From my experience, working towards anti-racism work this works well as a collaborative approach with the senior leaders, middle managers and an organization's diversity specialist and HR specialists. However, for smaller organizations the participation of senior leaders and decision-makers, accompanied with a commitment to a transformation approach to racial equity in itself, is also a good start.

REFLECTIONS TO SUPPORT GOOD PRACTICE AND WHAT TO AVOID

Organizations:

- Have you identified where you are and where you want to be as an organization?
- Have you thought about what an anti-racist approach looks like for your organization?
- Can you identify your 'must-do' priority actions and your 'nice-to-have' actions on the basis of evidence, data and information, not on what is trending on social media, to allow you to manage time and resources effectively?
- Are you honest in your discussions with staff about the approach that is to be taken? A transactional approach is not inappropriate if that's what you feel is better for your organization; however, be clear this approach is limited and will have very little impact in achieving racial equity or challenge the status quo.
- Are senior leaders and middle managers engaged and on board? Without this, it will be a challenge.
- Do middle managers understand their role in creating an organization that is fair and antiracist?

- Can you reframe your vision and commitment to an anti-racist transformational approach and engage with your employees?
- Consider what is needed to do to make sure the work you carry out is anti-racist. This can include policy development, recruitment practices, setting criteria for regulating individuals and so on.
- Have you engaged with your employee networks and other key groups/individuals about what you would like to achieve, where your gaps are and how they can support?
- Is your focus on doing the work rather than writing the words? The data and evidence following transformational approach will speak for itself over time – people are looking to see outcomes not read strategies.
- Are you bold, brave and willing to try something new? Remember, the work carried out on race equity to date comes with limited success – it needs something new. You are much more likely to be successful and respected for making changes to the way you work rather than for holding another event to discuss race equality/equity.

Avoid

- Holding events that lead to no action. If you do hold an event – what follow up action is there? Are you learning from what was shared and discussed and addressing it in your plans?
- Sticking to the similar actions that have failed to yield the outcomes desired.
- Avoid burdening Black and Brown people, employee networks with the responsibility of making progress.

What does a transformational approach look like?

What are the key factors to consider in adopting a transformational approach? Here are some suggestions that I provide detail on below:

- Stop asking Black and Brown people to speak about their experiences.

- Be open, honest and act with integrity.

- Move beyond the business-case narrative.

- Provide good-quality and meaningful education and training.

- Take a data break.

- Recruit powerful and proactive allies.

Stop asking people of colour to speak

What I observed in the time following George Floyd's murder was Black people being called upon to share their experiences of racism. People were being asked to share their stories, to bare their souls and to show vulnerability. 'What is it like being Black at work?', 'How did George Floyd impact on you?', 'What should organizations do to improve race equality?', 'How can we increase our workforce so it is more representative?', 'How can we talk about race?'. These are a handful of questions we expect Black people to respond to and discuss.

Racism is not new; yet, since the killing of George Floyd there has been a sudden pique in interest in 'the Black experience'. I couldn't agree more with Ijeoma Olua in her book *So You Want to Talk About Race*[2] when she says, 'These are very stressful times for people of color who have been fighting and yelling and trying to protect themselves from a world that doesn't care, to suddenly being asked by those who've ignored them for so long, "What has been happening your entire life? Can you educate me?"'[3] Black and Brown people are not responsible for educating others on racism. Should you want to find it, information about the experience of people of colour is available and has been for some time now.

Asking Black and Brown people to speak is nothing new and most organizations that celebrate Black History Month annually will showcase Black talent and ask Black people to attend and contribute to panel discussions. However, we must remember that this comes with a measure of pain and trauma.[4] When people do share their stories, I find it to be most discourteous: a) to scrutinize the facts and/or play devil's advocate, offering a different perspective on the racism that occurred; and b) when what has been shared has not been reflected on in relation to changes and a positive course of action beyond the individual transactional approach. Individual accounts of endured racism are powerful to some extent; they allow us to sympathize and can be eye-opening and, while this has some value, it really doesn't get to the point of racism, how it manifests and continues to exist. It is not the individual acts of racism that need to be spotlighted but rather, as I have discussed previously, the structure and the people who allow it to continue. However, Black and Brown people rarely contribute to panel discussions about addressing and dismantling a system of oppression, in my opinion for fear of repercussions. Instead, I see Black and Brown people, unwittingly in some cases, being used as fodder to somehow distract from the real systemic problems.

Individual transactional approaches do very little to progress race equity or to address the differential outcomes. Of course, dialogue about racism must continue; however, it is important to think about how this takes place effectively and among whom. It is not Black and Brown people that need to be engaging in these conversations among themselves or amongst good allies, it is those in power with influence that do – mainly senior leaders. The closest analogy that comes to mind when talking about institutional and organizational racism, structures and oppression is of a disabled person sharing their experiences of buildings lacking accessibility; the disabled individual can share their story and countless difficulties they have encountered, the humiliation and the anecdotes of having been picked up literally and taken into a building and so on; listeners will sympathize with that individual; they may even be angered that the building was not accessible; a lift may even be put into that organization. However, unless accessibility is considered as part of the design and construction for all buildings at planning stages, that individual and others will continue to face the same challenges wherever they go. To create an accessible world in this regard you would literally have to reconstruct every building. Any discussion about the barriers that disabled people experience must also include discussion about the design of buildings and accessibility to architects, planners and other relevant agencies. That's exactly what I feel is required to address inequality for Black and Brown people. There is little point in Black and Brown people speaking if organizations are not willing to listen and take appropriate action at the right level.

When Black and Brown people *do* speak it is important to listen. I recall writing a response to an organization following an invitation for suggestions to improve on diversity. I had drafted and redrafted my response in relation to improvements that could be made to achieve inclusion and equity and it took longer than it ever really should have. I asked a friend to read over what I had written to cross-check that my tone was friendly, constructive and supportive – that it couldn't be misconstrued as unhelpful or super-critical. However, despite my care and sensitivity, the suggestions were not received positively, and I was met with a defensive stance and a negative shift in our interactions from then on. I feel when Black and Brown people are invited to share and to come forward there are some unspoken rules: it must be in a manner that does not make anyone feel uncomfortable; in addition, there is a need to be hyper-vigilant and mindful of the emotional wellbeing of white people – for most Black and Brown people (I have most certainly felt this) it comes at the expense of our own wellbeing. Robin DiAngelo[5] contends that white people are socialized into a deeply internalized sense of superiority that they are either unaware of or don't like to admit to. Of course, then, the converse, it could be argued, is that Black and Brown people are socialized into a deep sense of inferiority perhaps? DiAngelo suggests that white people become highly fragile in conversations about race and this stems from entitlement and superiority. The media coverage in recent months debating whether the UK is racist has perhaps supported her suggestions. The platform afforded to Black and Brown people shouldn't come without boundaries and restrictions. Unless you are going to listen and take action, don't ask Black and Brown people to speak on racism and everything that comes with it.

For Black and Brown people, racial identity and all that goes with are integral to daily life. There is a constant reminder that racism exists: for me and most people I have spoken to over the years it is when we walk into a room and we are the only Black and Brown person; when we see a panel of speakers and there is no Black and Brown people represented; when it is reported that there is underrepresentation of people of colour in senior positions in most organizations; when there is an attainment gap in education; when we are murdered because of the colour of our skin; when there are barriers put in place to limit our growth in relation to career progression and success; when we are at higher risks of being affected by viruses; when we are more likely to die during labour – and so on. These are all-encompassing elements of the daily lives of Black and Brown people and cannot be separated into distinct, neat boxes to be opened when it is suitable for the majority. For most Black and Brown people, race has always been on the agenda, and many have spoken about it publicly; it is just now, people are pushed to listen. Most Black and Brown people have been speaking about this privately for many years in our homes, with our families and children, with our peers and with our colleagues offline. Some of us are exhausted and are reluctant to speak about it openly, especially if there are few positive and demonstrable outcomes as a result.

REFLECTIONS TO SUPPORT GOOD PRACTICE AND WHAT TO AVOID

Organizations:

- Do you have people that are specifically tasked with bringing about cultural and organizational change? As with most areas of work, success and achievements come with investing in expertise and professionals. Black and Brown people are not specialists in bringing about cultural and organizational change (unless they are in those roles). Today, there any many well-informed and respected individuals and organizations that can speak and educate on anti-racist practice – use them.
- Welcome those who come forward to speak about their experiences – listen and ensure you follow it up with action that leads to tangible outcomes as mentioned previously.

Avoid

- Avoid taking a defensive stance when Black and Brown people share their experiences or thoughts. Listen with empathy, compassion and kindness. Remember that for some Black and Brown people, speaking and providing feedback takes courage and comes with a sense of vulnerability and emotional tax.

Be open, honest and act with integrity

I am often challenged with suggestions that more time is needed for real progress to take place; I hear that organizations are most certainly committed, that race equality is important to them and they are having really good conversations about race. I also hear well-meaning individual senior leaders profess their commitment and passion for equality, yet most fail to take any real proactive action that leads to good outcomes. Senior leaders may attend or chair an event – however, with nothing much afterwards. There are individuals who take an anti-racist stance and become the face of equality, but these few are not sufficient for change.

The Race Relations Act emerged in the 1960s and racial inequality is not new. Let us be open and frank about the lack of progress to date. This is not an attempt to beat organizations with a stick, more to demonstrate that there is a shared understanding between Black and Brown people and organizations of the true state of play. I am sure most Black and Brown people see beyond the veneered narrative that is quite often spun. Organizations are much more likely to gain support and buy-in from everyone when they are open and honest. Trying to push forward a positive spin, in my view, lacks integrity and respect, the very thing that most organizations pride themselves on through their values and mission statements. It is important to measure progress *honestly* and to be honest about your starting point, what you have done and where you want to get to. This will also help to manage budgets and resources, allowing you to identify the practical next steps organizations can take. Too often I see resources being ploughed into events, discussions, and other similar activities that don't address any of the problems we discuss here in this book. When a strategy is built around honesty and progress is measured using data, whether qualitative or quantitative, it allows for resources to be allocated appropriately, bringing benefits with it. Anything else looks superficial and orchestrated for marketing purposes.

REFLECTIONS TO SUPPORT GOOD PRACTICE AND WHAT TO AVOID

Organizations:

- Are senior leaders going beyond chairing meetings and attending panel events? How are senior leaders supporting change? Are they holding people to account? Asking for data reports? Insisting a change in approach that leads to a positive outcome evidenced in data?
- Are senior leaders honest about the lack of progress to date and about future action you will take?
- Is progress measured in relation to data and information that is qualitative and quantitative? For example, your initiatives should see an increase in the number of Black and Brown people in senior positions or attaining higher degrees, or Black and Brown people should feel they are able to be themselves – evidenced by your employee attitude surveys for example.
- Are you engaging with your employee networks and Black and Brown people on what they think about the progress that has been made and use this as one of the indicators of success?
- Are you open about the challenges that you face as an organization? To gain support be open and bold even if this may be uncomfortable.

Avoid

- Engaging in activities that are not related to the improvements you want to see for example, holding yet another event – use your resources wisely.
- Putting forward senior champions as allies if they are not willing to put the time in and do the work.

- Bullshitting! – often carefully chosen words used to obscure progress are ironically transparent; you will lose trust and integrity.

Beyond the business case

The case for race equality is held hostage to potential economic gain. Most organizations are well versed in the business case for racial diversity and the moral case is glossed over as a given. But more attention should be paid to the 'right thing to do'. For race to be taken seriously, it seems that we must promote the 'business benefits' and influence senior leaders into appreciating what can be gained economically to improve the bottom line and enhance overall performance. Though there is a lack of conclusive evidence for the diversity 'business case', with both positive and negative outcomes of diverse teams being a possibility,[6] the business case is thrust forward as a strong argument. It seems that Black and Brown people must bring something more to the organization and most reports and discussion on race reference these gains. Baroness McGregor Smith, in her review made this point well in the section 'The reward is huge'. She goes on to state that, 'If BME talent was to be fully utilised, the economy could receive a £24 billion boost'[7] – 1.3 per cent GDP – that is £481 million a week,[8] and organizations with more diverse teams have 36 per cent better financial returns.[9] The push to sell the business benefits sits rather uncomfortably with me. Britain's colonial past is rooted in the desire for economic gain (and exploitation) and this feels rather similar. Black and Brown people should be employed, bought into boards and join senior teams, both because of the gains that are to be achieved across the board and because it addresses years of inequality. This business case narrative that is so often used makes me feel much like a commodity. We should be invested in the notion that everyone should have equal rights and opportunities with equitable outcomes – the commercial gain being the pleasing by-product rather than the ultimate motivation. If financial profit could be gained from all-white, male boards and senior leadership teams, would we want to be advocating this position? No, of course not. The 'strong business benefits' of racial diversity should not be the driving force. Rather, organizations should be making sure their company values and vision that are so readily displayed on their websites and the like match their commitment and actions. The aim here is one of humanity, justice and fairness, not one of being on trial and accepted only when the majority deems it acceptable and beneficial to do so.

REFLECTIONS TO SUPPORT GOOD PRACTICE AND WHAT TO AVOID

- Are senior leaders promoting the narrative that racial diversity is a necessary requirement if the organization believes in equity and equality for all?

Avoid

- Relying on the business case – we must move beyond that.

Education, learning and development

The purpose of any training in an organization is to raise awareness and educate to change for the better and improve performance, in addition to instilling the right skills, behaviours and attitudes. The purpose of learning, to some extent, is to raise awareness too. However, raising awareness alone does nothing if it is not accompanied by action to bring about change.

Activities such as events, discussion and initiatives that are based on sharing experiences are rarely effective in eliminating racism of the institutional and structural kind, assuming that is the aim here. If the aim of the training is simply to raise awareness without resulting in change to tick the training box; well, I have no words.

I appreciate the legal requirements imposed on organizations to provide training to their employees, not least because legal protection is a necessary requirement; however, this is in no way a real and practical educational route to understanding racism, and therefore developing anti-racist ways of working.

It is essential that any training includes the following focal points:

- race as a social construct and racism as a result;

- the history of race and whiteness and white supremacy and how they show up in institutes and organizations;

- addressing white supremacy as a system of oppression at an organizational level;

- bias, stereotypes, prejudice and discrimination and the systems in place to address these at an organizational level;

- allyship and how to do it; and

- the impact of racism on policy-making and on business as usual.

The problem with unconscious bias training

As briefly mentioned in Chapter 2 there has been a growing trend and interest amid many organizations post-George Floyd to advance their work on race by providing unconscious bias training. The training has intended to provide awareness of the many biases that individuals hold unconsciously (although there are also conscious ones we hold too) in addition to other contributing factors, such as prejudice and stereotyping. However, in recent times this has come with some criticism. Unconscious bias training is useful in helping individuals understand discrete biases, particularly as we all have them, and they are intrinsic to how we make sense of the world around us. However, this transactional approach that places emphasis on the individual does little to address bias, and ultimately, racial inequality. I am not suggesting that unconscious bias training should no longer be delivered; in fact, I think it provides a good understanding of personal biases. However, to address and reduce bias it is necessary to change the deep-rooted bias that resides in policies, practices and systems at an organizational level. If the way in which an organization is set up does not allow people of colour to succeed, if the policies and criteria result in an adverse impact for people of colour, this suggests unfair bias in those policies. Therefore, while one might be aware and make one's best efforts to partake in objective decision-making at a micro level following unconscious bias training – be aware and acknowledge this does little for advancing racial equity if the systems continue as they are.

REFLECTIONS TO SUPPORT GOOD PRACTICE AND WHAT TO AVOID

- Do your learning interventions go beyond the basic concepts of equality, equity diversity and inclusion and are race-specific?
- Does your learning explore the history of racism, its origins and power, as this provides context and understanding to any action?
- Does learning allow your organization to grow and challenge its current working practices with the aim of change? – if not, is it a tick-box exercise?
- Is the impact and effectiveness of training and learning opportunities in direct relation to your data on disparities

and disproportionality? If there is a continuing trend following learning interventions, it is most likely that the training has been ineffective.
- Are there a range of resources that can provide learning opportunities beyond traditional training? This can include book clubs, podcast clubs and/or discussion groups.
- Do senior leaders receive appropriate learning for the roles they hold and how to drive change.

Avoid

- Avoid training that is too general and fails to take into consideration the organizational needs, target audience and outcomes to be achieved.
- Training that does not go beyond equality legislation. Whilst it is important to understand the legal context organizations need much more to drive cultural change.
- Asking Black and Brown people to educate you on racism and everything that goes with it. Ask experienced specialists/ experts to support your agenda and to provide the learning you require.

Take a data break

Data and research are vital in understanding the progress to date and the gaps and inequalities that exist in every sphere of society. Of course, there is great value in data, but I feel we have got to a point where we have what we need. Organizations carry out detailed analysis and/or academic research to better understand the factors that contribute to racial inequality. This is useful, however, in principle and at a high level, they come to similar conclusions for Black and Brown people in most cases. For example, the report, 'Healing a Divided Britain: The Need For a Comprehensive Race Equality Strategy' by the Equalities and Human Rights Commission[10] found the following in employment and education:

- *Employment*

Black workers with degrees earn 23.1 per cent less on average than White workers in Britain, significantly lower percentages of ethnic minorities (8.8 per cent) worked as managers, directors and senior officials, compared with white people (10.7 per cent) and this was particularly true for African or Caribbean or Black people (5.7 per cent) and those of mixed ethnicity (7.2 per cent).

Black people who leave school with A-levels typically get paid 14.3 per cent less than their white peers.

- *Education:*

Just 6 per cent of Black school leavers attended a Russell Group university, compared with 12 per cent of mixed and Asian school leavers and 11 per cent of white school leavers.

Black Caribbean and mixed white/Black Caribbean children have rates of permanent exclusion about three times that of the pupil population as a whole.[11]

As I have mentioned previously, most data at an organizational level will not deviate too far from the above, and the running themes are all so similar. There seems to be a fixation with collating additional information at a more granular level to further understand and appreciate every nuance. However, I suggest moving away from data for a while and working on the principle that organizations need to make every effort to address racial inequality via several transformational *actions*. I frequently wonder if the additional and sometimes never-ending commissioning of research, qualitative or quantitate, is simply a strategic move to redirect focus. It provides the illusion that work is underway, in the absence of actually delivering direct change and positive outcomes for Black and Brown people. Further research at an organizational level, while interesting and providing sector-specific information that is nuanced to that organization, does not really tell a different story. To my knowledge, the research and/or recommendations to date have not led to racial equity; therefore, I suggest organizations move away from being so data-focused (assuming you have a level of data already) and taking a data break – most organizations have what is required. It's time to start the work.

REFLECTIONS TO SUPPORT GOOD PRACTICE AND WHAT TO AVOID

- Have you identified the information and data you already have and what is available nationally and considered if you are able to work with that? It is far better to use your resources to put measures in place than to use them to carry out more research.
- Do you have an action plan that specifically addresses the gaps in your organization? Remember research is a tool to support your anti-racist work. It is not a means to an end. Much money can be plugged into research; however, significant changes to policy and structures need to take place to achieve racial equality and equity.
- Are you able to use your resources into actions?
- Think about carrying out research if you have nothing to get you started on your anti-racist practice – this can include qualitative and quantitative.

Avoid

- Carrying out research to explain away racism and support a narrative that you may want to put forward.

White allies

White people are the gatekeepers to progress. They have the ability and power to either contribute to racial equity or racial inequality. Just as the global movement HeForShe[12] is a powerful platform for men to speak against inequality for women, white allies are a powerful tool for people of colour. The most powerful allies are senior leaders and middle managers.

What is an ally in this context?

An ally:

- is someone who in their daily conduct continuously challenges the racial inequality that exists and understands that something more than an individual approach is required to address racism at work;

- understands the system of whiteness and oppression and works to raise awareness of this;

- is comfortable talking about race and is open to listening and learning;

- is someone who works to build genuine trusting relationships with people of colour;

- is willing to do the work to increase their understanding and does not rely on people of colour to educate them;

- understands that this is not about individual white people but a system; and

- supports people of colour and understands the privilege they hold (through no doing of their own).

The best allies are those who are proactive in addressing and challenging racism and working to dismantle it in all spaces and spheres, from recruitment and policy and decision-making to outside of work in informal settings such as family gatherings and events.

REFLECTIONS TO SUPPORT GOOD PRACTICE AND WHAT TO AVOID

- Do you have a good understanding on the history of racism, 'whiteness' and privilege? A good understanding of this will help you to support others.
- Do you show compassion and kindness towards people who share their experiences with you and use your privilege and influence to speak out and against barriers?
- Do you show your commitment to anti-racism by challenging policies that do not allow, or make it harder for Black and Brown people to thrive and flourish?
- Are you committed to doing the work? Remember allyship is not a campaign or a momentary initiative; it requires commitment and long-term practice and work.

Avoid

- Becoming an ally for PR and marketing purposes – you want to be respected and trusted.

- Leaving it to people of colour to address racism and racist incidents and to challenge structures.
- Assuming you know how people of colour feel – be open to learning.

USEFUL RESOURCES FOR ALLIES

These webpages have some great links to videos and books:

'Resources for Aspiring White Allies & Accomplices', *Make Work More Human,* https://www.makeworkmorehuman.com/white-ally-resources

'Dr Robin DiAngelo discusses "White Fragility"', *YouTube,* https://www.youtube.com/watch?v=45ey4jgoxeU

'How to be an Antiracist', *YouTube,* https://www.youtube.com/watch?v=TzuOlyyQlug

Ibram X. Kendi (author of *How to Be an Antiracist*) at the FYE® Conference 2020, *YouTube,* https://www.youtube.com/watch?v=doHhMjudb3c

Ibram X. Kendi, 'The difference between being "not racist" and antiracist' *YouTube,* https://www.youtube.com/watch?v=KCxbl5QgFZw

Nita Mosby Tyler, 'What if white people led the charge to end racism?' | TEDxMileHigh, *YouTube,* https://www.youtube.com/watch?v=VQSW5SFBsOg

6

WHY AREN'T THINGS CHANGING?

Aseia Rafique

Introduction

Is it that we are comfortable with where we are, the status quo that we think holds things together – for now? Perhaps, but it is the structures and processes, systems and culture, religion and dogma, which provide space for bias that are the places and spaces which we need to interrogate. The norms by which we live are deeply ingrained, so much so that it is difficult and sometimes impossible to push through to bring about meaningful change. We are all caught in this – often believing that the right way to behave and to do things is the way we do them ourselves. This is why seismic shifts such as Black Lives Matter and the #MeToo campaigns are forcing others to look at issues through the lens of other people. What we don't understand, we dismiss, or we look to others, rightly or wrongly, to validate our choices and behaviours.

There are a lot of answers to a question about 'why aren't things changing' but they are not easy explanations. And things *are* changing, albeit very slowly, and generally only when there is the political will to do so. The dynamics of race and society and its many iterations and interactions feed into the complexities and intersections of who we are – of race, identity, class and other characteristics.

One of the things I find alarming is that discussions that talk about race, equity and that look to engage people on how we can provide a better quality of life for those who are under-represented, marginalized or from less-privileged backgrounds become so politicized, so quickly. This is one of the challenges of why things aren't changing quickly enough. Some of India's most impoverished people, the Dalits or 'Untouchables', for example, are part of a caste system which is perhaps the world's longest-surviving social hierarchy. This is a community that belongs to the lowest caste in India, and is trapped in a cycle of poverty and exclusion. Such illegal, yet culturally ingrained caste discrimination means that Dalits remain the most oppressed community in India. Having watched the BBC series *India* with Sanjeev Bhaskar, I was struck when Sanjeev was taken into a neighbourhood where whole families were busy recycling the rubbish they collect from wealthier neighbourhoods – newspapers, bottles, clothes and the like. 'I don't ever come here,' the co-presenter says to Sanjeev, and in that one sentence, I saw how having caste privilege benefits the millions who are born into one of the 'better', more privileged castes. Bias and inequity happens because it benefits those who are in positions of privilege and power, and those who have privilege and power are loathe to change the status quo because of the benefits afforded to them. I mean, who else is going to do the dirty work?

Identity politics – blocking the change we want to see

There are multiple factors that keep bias alive – one of which is the politicization of race and identity and the emergence of identity politics. Perceptions and ideas of identity, race, ethnicity and religion are constantly debated, eliciting ever-growing, polarized opinions – and identity politics, unfortunately, has become the new catchphrase for everything that is not quite right in our society today. But what is identity politics, and why does it create so much controversy? That people want to see change in the way they live their lives; that they want to have access to opportunities and be able to make the choices they want in a way that works best for them – I mean that shouldn't be too much to ask, should it? But what is stopping people having their lives they want to live? Right now we have a society that works better for some people than others. That we live in a racialized society may be for some an extreme view to take, but no parent should have to explain to their children that because they are Black or Brown, or because they are a Black or Brown girl they will have to work ten times harder than their white peers to make it. Why? They just might be thought of as a troublemaker or asked to take time out of school if they have the 'wrong' hairstyle or are wearing the wrong kind of uniform or are subject to racist 'banter'.

Identity politics focuses on trying to achieve change that speaks to people's identity and on such social issues such as the over-criminalization of young Black men, decolonizing the curriculum, discussions about rape, cancel culture, the fluidity of gender for those that identify as LGBTQ+ and trans people in bathrooms. These and other topics seem to produce highly inflammatory opinions, but what is missing in all these disagreements is having a conversation about such subjects. These topics are heavily debated on social media and there are many attempts to attack others who do not agree.

Those arguing for change feel as if the emphasis should be on addressing historical injustices as well as looking at systemic racism and bias in our systems – in health care, education and policing for example. On the other side of the debate is whether people want to believe that structural bias, historical or otherwise even exists. And if bias is present, it is reasoned that it is the fault of a few bad apples rather than structures and systems. This two-sided debate has one side that wants to preserve the status quo, histori-cally protecting a white identity that many white, male, cisgender people identify with. The other side sets out the concerns, issues and bias minority groups face, presented as dangerous (it is not the police's fault if young Black men engage in knife crime) – or too woke – (students cancelling talks from representatives they do not agree with) – or too militant – (protesting against historical injustices is un-British).

Those arguing against identity politics believe that fault lies with the individual and not the system. And when politicians and others wade in, not only do the fault lines deepen but it creates a perception that the changes people are asking for are wrong and unjust. Such views create headlines, but do not stop to articulate *why* people are demanding change. It is not – even if people think it is – about removing white authors from the curriculum, but about adding in and including other diverse voices in the spaces we inhabit. Such arguments simply help to obfuscate the real challenges and, cynically, I believe it is one of the reasons why things aren't changing. Pretending there are no problems, or the problems are related to individuals rather than societal issues helps preserve the power and privilege of those who already have it. Even when historians and museums decide to look at and document historical injustices and to change and reference such points in their work, they are labelled as 'going too far', or cancelling out 'real' history. Whiteness matters and it matters more than Brownness and Blackness.

In conversations about identity and race, white identity is rarely mentioned or discussed. This is simply because whiteness is seen as the default and the norm. Whiteness is usually absent when we talk about race – but it is a huge part of the conversation around identity politics. You might not believe it but white identity can even determine outcomes of elections. Think Donald Trump, and issues of immigration, or Nigel Farage and his poster showing a queue of immigrants lining up to come to Britain before the Brexit vote.

And although Britain is less overtly racist than it was fifty years ago, many minority groups still face racism. We live in a culture, however, where you either believe that Britain has some way to go to support minority populations or that we are already where we want to be. Improvements are made and laws passed, but we are not there yet. Terry Smith in *Unmasking White Grievance at the Ballot Box*[1] in America explained that voters do, in fact, discriminate on the basis of race. Smith argues that such decision-making, where people vote on the basis of race, is unlawful and that voters should be protected from political candidates who use racism and racial stereotyping to advance their policies. This may not be a way to overcome white grievance, but it shows that even in their voting preferences, there are huge cultural, political and racial divides among us. The problem is that there is a real discomfort in talking about the racialized nature of how people make decisions and how they see the world. And where white privilege is challenged, and whiteness is seen as the default standard of power or value, then white grievance is an inevitable by-product. The grievance politics of gender and race has, unfortunately, led to division and animosity, with some white people seeing themselves as an embattled race, and increasingly viewing their economic and social condition in opposition to Black and Brown people. It's a shame because there are many shared experiences that people have and especially when it comes to hardship, deprivation or coming from a working-class background.

And it is whiteness – often labelled as working-class whiteness – that we are told is the most threatening or that it is these people that feel most threatened by race. This is what we saw when working-class men came to 'protect' the country's statues following the removal of Edward Colston's statue in Bristol. The narrative provided was one of white men drinking, shouting and urinating. But these white working-class folk are not the gatekeepers of change. They help to visualize the discontent of others but as with any community, there are many, many others who support, live next to and get on with life with those around them. It is those in power who have power to enable change, and who continue to refuse to do so.

Colston's statue itself has been the subject of increasing controversy since the 1990s, when his work as a philanthropist came under scrutiny due to his involvement in the Atlantic slave trade. More recently, in 2018, there was an effort to reword the plaque to include details of Colston's role in the slave trade. These efforts to change what was written on the plaque were rejected. And it was the local authority officials rejecting the change – it was the people in power who said no. Now, however, the debate on the removal of statues or the changing of place names or street names has become mired in sentiments around who is really British and who isn't? If you were *truly* British, you would not want to change history and remove such historical figures and would understand the importance of keeping such figures erected. But as Afua Hirsch[2] and others have pointed out, as a Black student at the University of Oxford, holding reverence to characters and figures who played key roles in the slave trade and the oppression of others, means discrediting the histories and realities of Black and Brown people today. But as some have said, let's not overly intellectualize racism. With more and more Black and Brown people 'refusing to know their place', this may be unfortunately what is bringing the bigots out of the woodwork.

Working-class whiteness in Britain came about when Black and Brown people arrived and with the arrival of non-white communities, the presence of working-class whiteness was thrust into the spotlight. Racism (and often much of society's other ills) is blamed as being propagated by working-class people in the absence of anyone else. The narrative, that racism developed out of a perceived competition between 'white residents' and 'non-white immigrants' for scarce resources, such as housing and jobs, may hold true to a degree but the racialization of politics plays a much larger role. Demonizing communities because they looked different or didn't understand what 'being British' meant was a role some politicians took up with relish. Whiteness was fetishized and idealized and whereas previously this upper-class whiteness was exported by those that had power and privilege across the Empire, suddenly credence was given to white working-class people in Britain to see themselves as better than the newly arrived Brown and Black people. But this has itself been a distraction from the racist policies and ideologies that have been put in place by the elite. Every single step in the push to end systemic racism – from the abolition of slavery to Black Lives Matter – is what is known as identity politics today. Creating a white working-class divide has not been something that has simply happened; it is in the interests of the system for there to be such a divide. It allows for the focus to be driven away from genuine issues, moving away from creating inclusivity and instead putting the blame on Black and Brown people.

The argument focuses on whether we should look at bias in society or simply continue to tackle the more 'important' and politically palatable views on creating more jobs, building more homes and encouraging those that are not working into work. There are many examples of people trying to ban speakers, or to change the language we use and, although this can be seen as political correctness gone too far, the real issue is about who we are, what we identify as and who we want to accept as a true Brit. Nish Kumar, a British-Asian comedian has been branded 'a dangerous lefty ghoul who gets criticized in the right-wing press and lambasted on social media as a bigot, a hater, someone who is anti-British, and who pour[s] scorn on Britain's achievements.'[3] He says, 'I can only surmise that being Brown has something to do with it, as the same level of vitriol or racism is not directed towards white comedians.'

One example I remember was on BBC *Question Time* at the time when the country was debating the 'Brexit' fallout from voting Leave. Someone mentioned that it would be an opportunity for those living outside the EU, from Asian and African subcontinents to come to Britain to work. The answer provided by a panel member was that if they thought that by restricting immigration from EU members meant other Brown and Black people would be welcome to come from overseas, then they hadn't realized what the true nature of Vote Leave really meant. It depends, therefore, on who you are and if you have the right credentials – meaning white credentials – to live in Britain. The more white, the more accepted you will be. Polish and other white European immigrants, for example, have this one advantage over other minority ethnic groups. For Poles, who started to arrive in Britain after World War I, it took but one generation for their whiteness to 'mix in' and for their accents to become 'acceptable'.

This is especially so when we see political leaders using race to divide and penalize communities and such politics feeds into the amorphous feeding ground of political discussion. The question is always what is the 'right kind' of Brit? And what does it mean to be a 'real' Brit. What governments and politicians try to obscure is how communities become marginalized in the first place, whether that is because of specific policies or poverty or even cultural traditions and practices. Everything plays its part including the systems we use which themselves perpetuate bias and discrimination. Simply placing the blame on communities because of 'their high crime rates' or 'their lack of progression into board and CEO positions', does not take into consideration poverty, police brutality and the unequal distribution of wealth and opportunities available between different groups. Being a true Brit is very often framed as being white, and whiteness has been exported across the world as a valuable commodity. Whiteness has become so normalized and coveted that we see everything from whitening creams, as mentioned earlier, being dubiously sold – so that Brown or Black people can look 'more appealing and attractive' and 'whiter', to eyelid surgery for South East Asians – so they can widen their eyes to look more European. Even hairstyles that show off straight, flowing locks are mainstream products aimed at the Black and Brown hair market, even though this 'straight' hair is taken from Black and Brown people themselves.

White grievance

There are also those happy to criticize minority experiences or movements such as BLM – either for being too violent, for trying to rewrite history, for being too radical and, for some, for just simply putting the spotlight on the lives and lived experiences of minority ethnic people. Who can forget the 'White Lives Matter' meme making the rounds or the 'WHITE LIVES MATTER' banner that was flown over the Etihad Stadium at the beginning of a City game in Burnley? I even saw a 'Horses' Lives Matter', a meme on Facebook, in response to an image of a police officer kicking a horse. The racist bias hiding in comments such as these shows the concern some people have with Black and Brown people asserting their grievances. But grievance is also a white issue.

Juliet Hooker describes the term white grievance in her article 'Black Protest/White Grievance: On the Problem of White Political Imaginations Not Shaped by Loss'.[4] White grievance is an increasingly popular right-wing opinion that asserts that if those that have been traditionally marginalized make societal gains or achieve a modicum of equity, it would mean fewer resources and opportunities for white people. But this focus on the 'problems' created by Black and Brown people is not only articulated by those on the extreme left or right, but through the everyday news stories we read, what we listen to and whom we talk to. For example, Black women in the UK are four times more likely to die in pregnancy or childbirth, statistics Vanisha has highlighted in Chapter 3, and in Sandwell and Birmingham it was found infant mortality rates were highest in deprived areas and among Black, Pakistani and Bangladeshi-heritage families. When listening to such discussions, I noted that the interviewer would mention deprivation and maybe health inequalities, but that their questions would inevitably come back to the small percentage of evidence suggesting that consanguinity, or babies born to couples who are related as second cousins or closer, was a factor in congenital abnormality, and consequently, in increasing the risks of infant mortality. Even when it was clear that this was part of the evidence highlighted by a report by the Health and Social Care Overview and Scrutiny Committee,[5] showing that the key factors were deprivation, ethnicity and health inequalities, the questioning on consanguinity would continue. The message was that, yes, perhaps deprivation *is* a factor, but the problem is the inappropriate relations between Brown parents that is the main factor in causing these deaths. Instead of looking or discussing the systemic biases that impact on care, the focus is on the issue perceived to be created by Brown people themselves.

Juliet Hooker[6] argues that 'in countries where racial diversity continues to increase, coming to terms with systemic racial injustice is the key to building equitable, unified societies.' However, white grievance comes to the fore when it is believed that societal gains for Black and Brown people mean there is less to go round for others. The other worry is about being 'left behind'. The perennial statement we just cannot shake off is 'they'll come and take our jobs' and is something I have heard from both minority people and white people. I was taken aback when a Brown person mentioned that there were too many Polish people arriving in the country and there would not be enough jobs or school places to go round. For someone who had travelled on the same journey as these newly arrived migrants, I was sad to hear the latent prejudice in their statement.

Why white and working class?

The term 'white working class' has become mainstream, used in particular to explain why white working-class boys are left behind in educational and work outcomes. Linking race to disadvantage experienced by poverty does not take into consideration other groups also experiencing the same issues. Working class has become somewhat synonymous with the term 'white', but working class is a state held by minority and white communities alike and although there may be additional concerns and disadvantage felt because of race, ultimately, being working class and everything that comes with that – for example, having to make ends meet, losing out on 'cultural capital', such as having a wide and diverse vocabulary, being able to play a musical instrument, or participating in formal sports activities, such as tennis or swimming. This is cultural capital that is considered worthwhile in applications for further education. Often working-class people do not have the networks and contacts to get a foot in the door of that career they may have wanted, and this is a situation, regardless of race, that any working-class person will experience. The documented problems that white, working-class children face have little to do with being white and mostly to do with being working class. At GCSEs, Black pupils receiving free school meals (FSM) – a proxy for poverty – score around 17 per cent less than Black students not on FSM.[7] So do Asian pupils. For white pupils, though, the gap is double – 34 per cent). Inequality between white communities, between working-class and middle-class communities is the real concern, rather than the perceived and often narrated disadvantage between minority and white communities.

But class has also become a racialized term and by using white working class to describe a particular social phenomenon, it has itself become tied up in the conversation of identity politics and used as a weapon to confirm that it is not only Black and Brown people that are suffering but that white people are suffering too.

The debate that arose when white children began underperforming became a national conversation and there have been many books written to try to explain the causes. The same debate wasn't held for Brown or Black children – other than to surmise that there was a lack of aspiration and ambition among those groups and that particular cultures lent themselves to aspirational black holes, such as Pakistani and Bangladeshi pupils, who routinely have poorer educational outcomes than other pupils. The history of migration, the regions people migrated from and parents' own literacy rates have been little discussed in such conversations. Culture, religion and community dynamics are much easier to pinpoint and blame. But the issue is about class as much as it is about race and now that white, working-class boys have joined their Black peers at the bottom (the GCSE scores for Black Caribbean and white British pupils on free school meals are virtually the same), there is little to infer about what does, in fact, cause such outcomes.

This rise of identity politics has meant we have shifted away from discussing inequality in relation to politics or class and that now it is about culture and individual identities. As the Sewell Report notes, we are less racist today than in recent years and knowing that progress is being made is something to be thankful for. Yet disparities exist – they haven't gone away. Even today the Sewell Report highlights that the causes of disadvantages faced by minority groups lie primarily with minority groups, and that social issues – including the complexity of interactions between race and class are reframed as moral choices and simply due to the localized behaviour of individuals. It is a divisive view to hold and although there is agreement that racial disadvantage 'often overlaps with social and class disadvantage', the question is, how have some minority groups done better than others and what advantages did they have? The answer for government and politicians is the role that 'family structures' and 'cultural traditions' play. This does have a bearing, but it is not and cannot be seen as the only factor for consideration as to why some groups perform better than others. We need also to look at longstanding inequalities and structural racism. It is not simply individual behaviour and attitudes that cause disparities to occur, but a multitude of complex factors at play. Bias or racism can be a catch-all explanation, but to understand the narrative of structural disadvantage and racial disparities, we need to examine the intersectional interplay of race, class, gender and other characteristics.

The questions about what is right and wrong for those who have the power and the 'keeping of traditions' – for example, 'this is how we've always done things so it must be right', is where bias breeds. When I was young, it felt like all the Muslim schoolgirls I knew were prohibited by their families, from learning how to swim. Such tired notions of respectability, couched in power and privilege, continue to survive which damages all of us. And such 'cultural or religious traditions' thrown back in the face of Brown and Black people to explain their lack of progress in education and employment further damages progress and equality.

Who holds the power and how is that power reinforced? We have seen Black and Brown communities settling in the UK and are constantly reminded about the ones that have integrated 'the most'. One of the measures of appropriate integration is educational attainment. Here, we think about the Chinese and Indian communities, who, as said often in the media, are 'compliant and hard-working'. We know intrinsically that the 'right' kind of community are those who hold 'British Values',[8] values taught to children at school – kindness, compassion, fairness, not just British Values, but actually, *human* values. These communities, perceived as being of less bother and trouble are tolerated and fare better, for example, than those 'troublesome' communities, in being less of a focus and less vilified in politics and the media. But they also have not been without their own struggles. When Covid-19 emerged as a virus that originated from Wuhan, China, bullying, discrimination and harassment of Chinese people suddenly peaked. It doesn't take much for that veneer, the glue that we imagine holds people and society together to disintegrate. Racism has never gone away. And if you're the right kind of foreigner, what that means is that you never complain and that your worth is measured by your silence. Amy Chua, the author of *Battle Hymn of the Tiger Mother* explains that people have become exclusive in their own oppression,[9] so as not to come into the limelight and further experience bias or harassment.

Get back in your box

The question, as always, is: 'what does it really mean to be me?' Having experience of disadvantage and oppression is unique to those who live it. However, no individual can change the system on their own. Reni Eddo-Lodge, in one episode of her podcast series *About Race* chatted with Farrukh Dhondy,[10] about welcoming activism under the umbrella of 'Blackness' – where people of colour: Asian, Black, African and others come together to fight for equality, rights and fairness. Today it feels like we have politicized Blackness to such an extent that the very thing that brought marginalized groups together, their colour, is now the thing that has split them apart and fragmented them. The British Black Panther movement that ran during the 1960s and 70s was, for example, inclusive of all Blackness – anyone of colour. Farrukh Dhondy, in conversation with Reni Eddo-Lodge talked about how 'there was no colourism in the Black Panther movement. There were supporters, associates, but the membership was basically Asian and Black.'

This has now become termed as 'political Blackness', where people from diverse backgrounds come together to highlight injustice. Now instead of political or a shared Blackness, which is how I like to describe it, what has materialized is identity politics. The notion, idea and perception of identity has seeped into the fabric of language and people's beliefs and stretched to the limit the very ideas of shared Blackness. I, as were others, was swept up into the Black Lives Matter protest, but identifying as South Asian, I felt I could not publicly give my voice to the injustices faced by Black people. Although our shared histories intersect with each other, my experience was not their experience. By speaking out, I felt I would be invalidating the lived experience of a community who are penalized and criminalized double that of South-Asian people simply because of their Blackness. Black people are nine times more likely to face stop and search than white people, for example.[11] My marginalization, it seemed, could not be felt together with theirs. We had reached a crunch point of focusing on specific histories and specific paths of marginalization, dividing individual communities further apart.

This fragmentation of identity has been used to split people further from one another. Chua believes that this 'new exclusivity is partly epistemological', claiming that out-group members cannot share in the knowledge possessed by in-group members ('You can't understand X because you are white'; 'You can't understand Y because you're not a woman'; 'You can't speak about Z because you're not queer'). The idea of 'cultural appropriation' insists, among other things, that 'these are our group's symbols, traditions, patrimony and out-group members have no right to them.' [12]

We are shouting at one another to get back into the box we belong in. White authors writing about characters from a background they do not share are suddenly vilified, people wearing and borrowing clothes from a culture not their own are shot down and identifying with items which do not originate from your own background or heritage is dismissed as cultural appropriation. Having respect for others and acknowledging other cultures in creative ventures is perhaps where all this has gone wrong.

The legacy of cultural appropriation has itself been one of winners with the losers being erased from history. It is not for nothing when we say, for example, that 'now that a white person has bought into that piece of music, that fashion garment, that story', suddenly it, that thing, has been validated. Grime music was banned, but as soon as it became more mainstream and a wider, more-white audience tuned in, it became acceptable. I remember a time when other people shouted abuse at me, telling me, 'I smelled of garlic', and then one day that very garlic was put on the school menu and suddenly it was OK. It is saddening and ironic that Black and Brown people feel the need to whiten up. Hair weaves,[13] hair straighteners, skin bleaching, double eyelids, height, colourism – i.e., prejudice against darker-skinned people or privileging lighter-skinned people, who are seen as superior because their skin is 'whiter' – are all ways in which we are looking to conform to a white, Eurocentric model. And not just in looks but behaviour as well. The whole mantra of being your whole self means that you should feel able to be expressive, loud and passionate, if that is who you are, but our lives are reined in and we are made to conform. Women have been carrying the emotional labour, a term given meaning by Arlie R Hochschild[14] as the unpaid, invisible work we do to keep things moving, keep the wheels oiled. Black and Brown people, similarly, have been keeping silent, agreeing and accepting a white narrative, just to keep their lives moving.

REFLECTIONS ON GOOD PRACTICE

- Take the time to understand other points of view.
- Offer your support to promote equality, diversity and inclusion.
- Have a conversation with others to discuss identity and what that means to different people.
- Write to your local MP and ask about anti-racist strategies.

Avoid

- Invalidating someone else's experience of racism by pretending it did not happen.
- Arguing or wading into debate about subjects you do not know anything about, or you have not had personal experience of.

Conclusion

Well, what's at stake? All of us want to live our best lives; to make sure our families and children are safe and to know that as we progress in our lives, in our education and careers, we do so with the knowledge that our choices and opportunities are not limited because of the colour of our skin. But we live in the real world, where structural and systemic racism is ignored. We either pretend it doesn't exist or we just don't take it seriously enough. And we live in a world where race and racism have become bywords for hate, and where discussing or mentioning experiences of bias and discrimination makes you not just an 'outsider' but an 'enemy of Britain'.

As human beings, who just happen to be different shades of black and brown, equitable access to education, housing, employment should be available to all of us. And where there are disparities, let's have a look and see what's happening. Let's look and make the changes that ultimately benefit everyone in society. This is not about taking from one group and giving to another – there is enough opportunity out there for all of us, I promise – it's about being honest. There is disparity and inequity in the world we live in, so let's acknowledge this and let's call it out. This is about empathy and understanding and, most of all, it's about leaving our prejudice and biases at the door – and at the doors of social media – when we move about in the world. We cannot understand every individual experience, but we can lobby and push for change, for ourselves and for others, no matter where any of us started in life. And you and I are those people that can help make a difference.

Identity politics has helped to inflame contemporary racist attitudes and bias. As Black and Brown people we are viewed through a lens of whiteness, which comes with many challenges. These challenges are not insignificant when death is a real possibility. While Derek Chauvin was found guilty of the murder of George Floyd, which some have cited as a turning point in history, let's not forget that Black people in the UK are twice as likely to die in police custody in England and Wales, Black and Asian women are respectively five times more likely and twice as likely to die during labour and the disproportionate impact of COVID-19 on Black and Asian people remains.

Differences in outcomes among minority ethnic groups continue to exist in employment, income and wealth, housing, education, criminal justice, health and other areas. And although many factors contribute to such differences, we cannot get away from structural and systemic racism as a major contributing factor for such differential and disproportionate outcomes. An explanation of racism of the structural kind seems to be tarnished with avoidance, anger and denial. Why is this the case? There is no single reason but depending on who you are, your seniority, your place in society, your political stance and allegiance and maybe even the colour of your skin – the reasons will vary. Some don't want to upset or make you feel uncomfortable or even alienate white people for fear of being 'othered', knowing the adverse impact this can bring. For others, the failure to address or acknowledge racism is a choice that brings benefits. And there are those who simply have no understanding and do not want to see what the rest of us have no choice but to see.

In the workplace, the many, and sometimes outdated attempts to create an equitable workplace and inclusion at all levels have been somewhat ineffective. For a fairer workplace and society, a different approach to diversity is required to the one that is adopted by most organizations, one which speaks from a place of honesty and vulnerability – honesty to accept these structures do not serve Black and Brown people and one that genuinely recognizes that progress is far too slow.

Racism and discrimination are predominantly, and perhaps even intentionally, concerned with relationships and personal interactions and it is easier to blame disparities on a lack of personal ambition or hard work. This absolves the guilty of accountability and pushes blame away from those who have the power to change it. The role of systems and structures must be brought to the forefront if we want to enable change in modern Britain and it is simply not acceptable for Black and Brown people to bear the load of dismantling racism. Being a person of colour does not come with innate competencies, insight and knowledge of structural racism, and there are Black and Brown people who deny that racism or structural inequity exist.

What does the future look like?

The future is equity and inclusion. We can have it if we want it. The recent events have highlighted racism and bias for what it is and the impact it has. If we can put people on the moon, send space crafts to Mars, invent smart phones that track location and other everyday inventions that make our lives easier, then we can change the way workplaces and societies are set up. We are making our way through a pandemic and to some extent carrying on with business as usual from our homes. Some of us were forced to turn our hands to home-schooling to deliver a curriculum and never thought in their wildest dreams they would need some level of knowledge on converting fractions into decimals. These changes to the way we usually did things, for example, going from working in the office to working online from home, did not take place overnight and required collective effort, desire and hard work. Therefore, if we want to, and if we want it, we can achieve ways of working that support most of us and we can reduce racism and discrimination. The lack of effort and political will only leads to the conclusion that it is not desired – if this is the case – cut the bullshit, the façade and the pretence and own it. It would save time, energy and resources, not to mention poor mental health outcomes for Black and Brown people. That said, for many of us, it is easy to spot those that are committed and those who pretend.

Is there hope? Absolutely! There is always hope. We would not be able to continue on this path of working with and in organizations as Diversity Specialists if we felt there was no prospect of change. There are many components that must come together to create an environment that supports and facilitates inclusion, equity and diversity and some of that foundation is ready to be built on. There are fantastic people, allies and senior leaders supporting this change, but it requires many more of us to do this.

Systems, structures and institutes do not exist in a vacuum; we are not dealing with fixed entities but constructs that can be changed should we wish to change them.

Endnotes

Chapter 1

1. Kim Knott, 'Moving People Changing Places: South Asians Making Britain', *Migration Histories*, 2011, https://movingpeoplechangingplaces.org/migration-histories/south-asians-making-britain.html [Accessed March 2021].

2. Enoch Powell, Keynote Presented at the General Meeting of the West Midlands Area Conservative Political Centre, Birmingham, 20 April, 1968, https://anth1001.files.wordpress.com/2014/04/enoch-powell_speech.pdf [Accessed September 2021].

3. GOV.UK, Ethnicity Facts and Figures: School Teacher Workforce, 18 February 2021, https://www.ethnicity-facts-figures.service.gov.uk/workforce-and-business [Accessed March 2021].

4. Akala, *Natives: Race and Class in the Ruins of Empire* (London: Two Roads, 2018).

5. Beverly Daniel Tatum, *'Why Are All the Black Kids Sitting Together in the Cafeteria?' and Other Conversations About Race* (New York: Basic Civitas Books, 2017).

6. Tatum, *'Why Are All the Black Kids Sitting Together in the Cafeteria?'* (2017), 133.

7. Tatum, *'Why Are All the Black Kids Sitting Together in the Cafeteria?'* (2017).

8. Ivan Smirnov and Stefan Thurner, 'Formation of Homophily in Academic Performance: Students Change Their Friends Rather Than Performance', *PLOS ONE*, 30 August 30 2017, https://journals.plos.org/plosone/article?id=10.1371/journal.pone.0183473 [Accessed April 2021].

9. Tatum, *'Why Are All the Black Kids Sitting Together in the Cafeteria?'* (2017), 155.

10. Christopher Paslay, 'What Is Whiteness?', *Inside White Fragility: A Critical Look at CRT and Education*, 2021, https://welcomingwhiteness.org/what-is-whiteness/ [Accessed April 2021].

11. Sean Coughlan, 'Only 1% of UK University Professors Are Black', *BBC News*, 19 January 2021, https://www.bbc.co.uk/news/education-55723120 [Accessed April 2021].

12. Pierre Bourdieu, *In Other Words: Essays Towards a Reflexive Sociology* – (Redwood City, CA: Stanford University Press, 1990).

13. Bourdieu, *In Other Words* (1990), 13.

14. Layla F Saad, *Me and White Supremacy: How to Recognise Your Privilege, Combat Racism and Change the World* (London: Quercus, 2020).

15. 'Tone policing is a tactic used by those who have privilege to silence those who do not by focusing on the tone of what is being said rather than the actual content.' Layla F Saad, *Me and White Supremacy* (2020), 46.

16. Saad, *Me and White Supremacy* (2020), 66.

17. Tatum, *'Why Are All the Black Kids Sitting Together in the Cafeteria?'* (2017), 180.

18. Carol Myers-Scotton and William Ury, 'Bilingual Strategies: The Social Functions of Code-Switching.' *Linguistics: An Interdisciplinary Journal of the Language Sciences* 15.193 (1977), 5–20. Also see Yaqub, 'Code Swtiching', *English Language Learning Forum*, 19 November 2009, https://englishlanguagelearningforum.blogspot. com/2009/11/code-switching.html [Accessed February 2021].

19. W E B Du Bois, *The Souls of Black Folk*, edited by Brent Hayes Edwards (Oxford: Oxford University Press, 2008).

20. W E B Du Bois, *The Souls of Black Folk* (2008).

21. Kwame Ture, Stokely Carmichael and Charles V Hamilton, *Black Power: The Politics of Liberation in America* (New York: Random House, 1988), 157.

22. Tatum, *'Why Are All the Black Kids Sitting Together in the Cafeteria?'* (2017), 175.

23. Resmaa Menakem, *My Grandmother's Hands: Racialized Trauma and the Pathway to Mending Our Hearts and Bodies* (London: Penguin, 2021).

24. Menakem, *My Grandmother's Hands* (2021), 103.

25. Rebecca Rogers and Melissa Mosley, 'Racial Literacy in a Second-Grade Classroom: Critical Race Theory, Whiteness Studies, and Literacy Research', *Reading Research Quarterly,* 41:4 (Oct–Dec 2006), 462–495 [Accessed March 2021].

26. *The Real McCoy* (TV series) https://www.bbc.co.uk/programmes/ p03oz4h5/episodes/guide [Accessed March 2021].

27. A genre of Jamaican music with an extensive use of Patois. See: https://en.wikipedia.org/wiki/Dancehall [Accessed March 2021].

28. Kyaien O Conner PhD, 'What Is Code-Switching?', *Psychology Today,* 3 December 2020 [Accessed March 2021].

29. Deloitte UK 'Respect and Inclusion', *Life at Deloitte*, https://www2.deloitte.com/uk/en/pages/careers/articles/respect-and-inclusion.html [Accessed February 2021].

30. Robin DiAngelo, *White Fragility: Why It's so Hard for White People to Talk About Racism* (Boston, MA: Beacon Press, 2018).

31. Barjinder Singh, Doan E. Winkel, and T. T. Selvarajan, 'Managing Diversity At Work: Does Psychological Safety Hold The Key To Racial Differences In Employee Performance?', *Journal of Occupational and Organizational Psychology*, 86: 2 (2013), 242–263 (London: Wiley). Kenneth B Clark and Mamie P Clark, 'Emotional Factors in Racial Identification and Preference in Negro Children', *The Journal of Negro Education*, 19:3 (1950): 341–50.

32. Louise Derman-Sparks and Patricia G Ramsey, 'What If All the Kids are White? Multicultural/Anti-Bias Education with White Children', 5:02 (2012), https://www.teachingforchange.org/wp-content/uploads/2012/08/ec_whatifallthekids_english.pdf [Accessed March 2021].

33. Kalwant Bhopal, *White Privilege the Myth of a Post-Racial Society* (Bristol: Policy Press, 2018), 21.

34. Menakem, *My Grandmother's Hands* (2021).

35. Peggy McIntosh, 'White Privilege: Unpacking the Invisible Knapsack', Peace and Freedom July/August 1989, https://psychology.umbc.edu/files/2016/10/White-Privilege_McIntosh-1989.pdf [Accessed April 2021].

36. McIntosh, *White Privilege* (1989).

37. McIntosh, *White Privilege* (1989).

38. Dr Tina Mistry, 'Brown Psychology', https://www.brownpsychologist.com/ [Accessed May 2021].

39. Menakem, *My Grandmother's Hands* (2021).

40. 'Racial equity is about applying justice and a little bit of common sense to a system that's been out of balance. When a system is out of balance, people of colour feel the impacts most acutely, but, to be clear, an imbalanced system makes all of us pay.' Glenn Harris, President, Race Forward and Publisher, Colorlines, 'What is Racial Equity?' Race Forward, https://www.raceforward.org/about/what-is-racial-equity [Accessed March 2021].

Chapter 2

1. Afua Hirsch, *Brit(ish) On Race, Identity and Belonging* (London: Penguin Random House, 2018), 19.
2. David Olusoga, *Black and British: A Forgotten History* (London: Macmillan, 2016), 8.
3. Amarpal Singh Sidhu, *The First Anglo-Sikh War* (Stroud: Amberley Publishing, 2013).
4. Arsh Behal, 'Sikh generals betrayal opened door for British', *Times of India*, 10 December 2017, https://timesofindia.indiatimes.com/city/chandigarh/sikh-generals-betrayal-opened-door-for-british/articleshow/62003378.cms [Accessed April 2021].
5. Akala, *Natives: Race and Class in the Ruins of Empire* (London: Two Roads, 2018).
6. GOV.UK, 'Commission on Race and Ethnic Disparities – Commission on Race and Ethnic Disparities: The Report' (March 2021), https://assets.publishing.service.gov.uk/government/uploads/system/uploads/attachment_data/file/974507/20210331_-_CRED_Report_-_FINAL_-_Web_Accessible.pdf [Accessed March 2021].
7. Rajeev Syal, 'Doreen Lawrence Says No 10 Report Gives "Racists the Green Light"', *The Guardian* (1 April 2021), https://www.theguardian.com/world/2021/apr/01/doreen-lawrence-says-no-10-report-gives-racists-the-green-light [Accessed April 2021].
8. Kenan Malik, *The Meaning of Race: Race, History and Culture in Western Society* (London: Palgrave, 1996).
9. Julian M Simpson, Aneez Esmail, Virinder S Kalra and Stephanie J Snow, 'Writing Migrants Back into NHS History: Addressing a "Collective Amnesia" and its Policy Implications', *Journal of the Royal Society of Medicine*, 103:10 (2010), 392–396.
10. Enoch Powell, 'Speeches and Articles', https://www.enochpowell.net/speeches.html.
11. Shazia Mirza, 'I'm a Comedian and Banter Is My Job – This Is the Truth about Racist Jokes', *The Guardian*, 9 November 2021, https://www.theguardian.com/commentisfree/2021/nov/09/british-banter-racism-yorkshire-cricket-row [Accessed November 2021].
12. Project Implicit, Harvard Implicit Association Tests, https://implicit.harvard.edu/implicit/takeatest.html [Accessed April 2021].
13. Definition from Oxford Languages, https://languages.oup.com/google-dictionary-en/ [Accessed April 2021].

14. Rupi Kaur, *Rupi Kaur Live* (2021), https://rupikaur.com/pages/about-me [Accessed April 2021].

15. Sam Friedman, Dave O'Brien, Ian McDonald, 'Deflecting Privilege: Class Identity and the Intergenerational Self', *Sociology*, 55:4 (January 2021), 716–733.

16. Akala, *Natives* (2018), 201.

17. Akala, *Natives* (2018), 23–37.

18. Speech by A. Sivanandan, Director of the Institute of Race Relations, on 1 November 2008.

Chapter 3

1. Peggy McIntosh, 'White Privilege: Unpacking the Invisible Knapsack', Peace and Freedom July/August 1989, https://psychology.umbc.edu/files/2016/10/White-Privilege_McIntosh-1989.pdf [Accessed January 2021].

2. GOV.UK, 'Race in the Workplace: The Time For Talking is Over: Now is the Time to Act', *The McGregor-Smith Review* (2021), https://assets.publishing.service.gov.uk/government/uploads/system/uploads/attachment_data/file/594336/race-in-workplace-mcgregor-smith-review.pdf [Accessed January 2021].

3. GOV.UK, 'Race in the Workplace' (2021), 2.

4. GOV.UK, 'The Stephen Lawrence Inquiry: Report of an Inquiry by Sir William MacPherson, Presented to Parliament by the Secretary of State for the Home Department by Command of Her Majesty, February 1999', Cm. 4262, https://assets.publishing.service.gov.uk/government/uploads/system/uploads/attachment_data/file/277111/4262.pdf [Accessed February 2021].

5. MacPherson Report (1999), 46:46.1.

6. Red Tape Challenge, https://www.gov.uk/government/news/red-tape-challenge [accessed November 2021].

7. https://assets.publishing.service.gov.uk/government/uploads/system/uploads/attachment_data/file/275769/dft-red-tape-challenge-highlights.pdf [Accessed November 2021].

8. Noah Uhrig, 'Black, Asian and Minority Ethnic disproportionality in the Criminal Justice System in England and Wales', Ministry of Justice Analytical Service 1 (2016), https://assets.publishing.service.gov.uk/government/uploads/system/uploads/attachment_data/file/639261/bame-disproportionality-in-the-cjs.pdf [Accessed May 2021].

9. Statista, 'Deaths in Police Custody in the UK 2019, by Ethnicity',

2019, https://www.statista.com/statistics/1122775/deaths-in-police-custody-in-the-uk-2019-by-ethnicity/ [Accessed April 2021].

10. This finding, and others using the general population in England and Wales as a comparator, may lead to a general conclusion that BAME individuals are always over-represented in the system when BAME individuals may or may not be over-represented at each CJS stage. See: 'Statistics on Race and the Criminal Justice System 2014: A Ministry of Justice Publication Under Section 95 of the Criminal Justice Act 1991' (2015) 68, https://www.gov.uk/government/uploads/system/uploads/attachment_data/file/480250/bulletin.pdf, [Accessed April 2021].

11. Bonhill Group, 'The DiversityQ FTSE 100 Board Diversity Report 2020' (2020) 12, https://s30776.pcdn.co/wp-content/uploads/2020/06/DiversityQ-FTSE100-report-20.final_.pdf [Accessed April 2021].

12. Bonhill Group, 'Board Diversity Report 2020'.

13. Universities UK, 'Black, Asian and Minority Ethnic Student Attainment at UK Universities: #closingthegap' (2019) 11, https://www.universitiesuk.ac.uk/sites/default/files/field/downloads/2021-07/bame-student-attainment.pdf [Accessed January 2021].

14. Tracey Bignall, Samir Jeraj, Emily Helsby and Jabeer Butt, 'Racial Disparities in Mental Health: Literature and Evidence Review', Race Equality Foundation (2021) 15, https://raceequalityfoundation.org.uk/wp-content/uploads/2020/03/mental-health-report-v5-2.pdf [Accessed April 2021].

15. GOV.UK, 'Detentions under the Mental Health Act', Detentions under the Mental Health Act, *Ethnicity Facts and Figures*, https://www.ethnicity-facts-figures.service.gov.uk/health/mental-health/detentions-under-the-mental-health-act/latest [Accessed February 2021].

16. GOV.UK, 'Disparities in the Risk and Outcomes of COVID-19', *Public Health England* (2020) 4, https://assets.publishing.service.gov.uk/government/uploads/system/uploads/attachment_data/file/908434/Disparities_in_the_risk_and_outcomes_of_COVID_August_2020_update.pdf, [Accessed April 2021].

17. ACEVO, 'Racial Diversity in the Charity Sector', 2018, https://www.acevo.org.uk/wp-content/uploads/2018/07/Racial-diversity-in-the-charity-sector.pdf [Accessed March 2021].

18. ACEVO, 'Racial Diversity in the Charity Sector' (2018).

19. NPEU, 'MBRRACE-UK Release: MBRRACE-UK: Saving Lives,

Improving Mothers' Care', 2018, https://www.npeu.ox.ac.uk/news/1642-mbrrace-uk-release-mbrrace-uk-saving-lives-improving-mothers-care?highlight=WyJmaXZlIHRpbWVzIlo= [Accessed March 2021].

20. MacPherson Report (1999), 6:4.
21. MacPherson Report (1999).
22. MacPherson Report (1999), 6:34.
23. Ellie Abraham, 'Racism Report: What is the Difference Between Institutional and Structural Racism?', *The Independent*, 1 April 2021, https://www.independent.co.uk/life-style/institutional-racism-structural-racism-report-b1825596.html, [Accessed February 2021].
24. Kehinde Andrews, in 'Racism Report: What is the Difference Between Institutional and Structural Racism?' the *Independent*, 1 April 2021, https://www.independent.co.uk/life-style/institutional-racism-structural-racism-report-b1825596.html [Accessed February 2021].
25. Layla F Saad, *Me and White Supremacy: How to Recognise Your Privilege, Combat Racism and Change the World* (London: Quercus, 2020), 12.
26. Ellis Cashmore and James Jennings (eds), *Racism and the Class Struggle: Further Pages From a Black Worker's Note Book From the Book Racism: Essential Readings* (London: Sage Publications, 2001), 130.
27. Kehinde Andrews, in 'Racism Report: What is the Difference Between Institutional and Structural Racism?' *The Independent*, 1 April 2021, https://www.independent.co.uk/life-style/institutional-racism-structural-racism-report-b1825596.html [Accessed February 2021].
28. Robin DiAngelo, *White Fragility: Why It's so Hard for White People to Talk About Racism* (Boston, MA: Beacon Press, 2018), 33.
29. Dr Stephen D. Ashe, Dr Magda Borkowska and Professor James Nazroo 'Racism Ruins Lives: An analysis of the 2016-2017 Trade Union Congress Racism at Work Survey', https://hummedia.manchester.ac.uk/institutes/code/research/projects/racism-at-work/tuc-full-report.pdf [Accessed December 2021].
30. Solicitor's Regulation Authority, Outcome of SDT Hearing, Samuel Maurice Charkham, 110194, 2020, https://www.sra.org.uk/consumers/solicitor-check/110194/ [Accessed March 2021].
31. Reni Eddo-Lodge, *Why I'm No Longer Talking to White People About Race* (London: Bloomsbury, 2017), 63–64.

32. Ian Law, Deborah Phillips and Laura Turnley (eds), *Institutional Racism in Higher Education* (Stoke-on-Trent: Trentham Books, 2004).
33. Eddo-Lodge, *Why I'm No Longer Talking* (2017).
34. DiAngelo, *White Fragility* (2018), 21.
35. Cashmore and Jennings, *Racism: Essential Readings* (2001).
36. Cashmore and Jennings, *Racism: Essential Readings* (2001), 13.
37. DiAngelo, *White Fragility* (2018).
38. DiAngelo, *White Fragility* (2018), 21.
39. Ijeoma Oluo, *So You Want to Talk About Race* (New York: Seal Press, 2020), 13.
40. Ijeoma Oluo, *So You Want to Talk About Race* (New York: Seal Press, 2020), 13.
41. DiAngelo, *White Fragility* (2018).
42. DiAngelo, *White Fragility* (2018), 57.
43. GOV.UK, 'Race in the Workplace', *The McGregor-Smith Review*, 2021.
44. Dr Doyin Atewologun and Roger Kline, with Margaret Ochieng, 'Fair to Refer? Reducing Disproportionality in Fitness to Practise Concerns Reported to the GMC', General Medical Council (June 2019), https://www.gmc-uk.org/-/media/documents/fair-to-refer-report_pdf-79011677.pdf [Accessed February 2021].
45. BAME contributions account for less than 10 per cent of the contributions made in the role of Production Executive (2.4 per cent), Series Producer (4.4 per cent), Head of Production (8.3 per cent) and Production Manager (9.3 per cent). 'Race and Ethnic Diversity: A Deep Dive into Diamond Data' (2020), https://creativediversitynetwork.com/wp-content/uploads/2020/10/RED-Full-Report-121020.pdf [Accessed February 2021].
46. Green Park, 'The Colour of Power', 27 July 2020, *Insights*, https://www.green-park.co.uk/insights/the-colour-of-power/s191468/ [Accessed March, 2021].
47. Green Park, 'The Colour of Power', 27 July 2020.
48. Green Park, 'The Colour of Power', 27 July 2020.
49. Green Park, 'The Colour of Power', 27 July 2020.
50. Eddo-Lodge (2017).
51. Eddo-Lodge (2017), 72.
52. Cashmore and Jennings, *Racism: Essential Readings* (2001), 223.
53. Yassmin Abdel-Magied and Mariam Khan, 'Open Letter to the BBC on Zara Mohammed's mistreatment on Woman's Hour', *gal-dem*, 2021, https://gal-dem.com/

open-letter-to-the-bbc-on-zara-mohammed-mistreatment-on-womans-hour/ [Accessed March 2021].

54. Tim Davie, 'Tim Davie's Response to Gal-Dem Open Letter' BBC Media Centre, 19 February 2021, https://www.bbc.co.uk/mediacentre/statements/tim-davie-response-gal-dem [Accessed March 2021].

55. 'Azeem Rafiq Still Receiving Abuse for Speaking Out in Yorkshire Racism Case', *The Guardian*, 4 November 2021, https://www.theguardian.com/sport/2021/nov/04/azeem-rafiq-says-institutional-racism-is-key-issue-after-gary-ballance-admits-racial-slur-cricket [Accessed November 2021].

56. Eddo-Lodge, *Why I'm No Longer Talking* (2017), 84.

57. Akala, *Natives: Race and Class in the Ruins of Empire* (London: Two Roads, 2018)

58. Akala, *Natives* (2018) 35.

Chapter 4

1. Ruby Hamad, *White Tears/Brown Scars: How White Feminism Betrays Women of Colour* (London: Trapeze, 2020), 1.

2. Koa Beck, *White Feminism* (London: Simon & Schuster UK, 2021).

3. Kimberlé Crenshaw, 'The Intersection of Race and Sex: A Black Feminist Critique of Antidiscrimination Doctrine, Feminist Theory and Antiracist Politics,' *University of Chicago Legal Forum*, 89:1 (1989), 139.

4. Sudarshan Abrol, Chair and Founder of the UK Asian Women's Centre, personal anecdote.

5. Alan Travis, 'Virginity tests for immigrants "reflected dark age prejudices" of 1970s Britain', *The Guardian*, 8 May 2011, https://www.theguardian.com/uk/2011/may/08/virginity-tests-immigrants-prejudices-britain [Accessed May 2021].

6. Pratibha Parmar, 'Gender, Race and Class: Asian Women in Resistance', in *The Empire Strikes Back: Race and Racism in 70s Britain* (London: Hutchinson, 1986), 245.

7. Nish Kumar, 'My name is Nish Kumar – so please stop calling me Nish Patel', *The Guardian*, 3 December 2018, https://www.theguardian.com/uk-news/2018/dec/03/my-name-is-nish-kumar-so-please-stop-calling-me-nish-patel [Accessed November 2021].

8. BBC Radio 4, *How To Be a Muslim Woman*, presented by Sayeeda Warsi, https://www.bbc.co.uk/

programmes/articles/x7GbC3ycnSqgK3H0Bryrf7/
why-we-need-to-change-the-way-we-talk-about-muslim-women.

9. 'Muslim Women Defy Ban to Swim in Burkinis at French Pool', *BBC News*, 24 June 2019, https://www.bbc.co.uk/news/world-europe-48744153 [Accessed November 2021].

10. 'Boris Johnson Faces Criticism over Burka "letter box" Jibe', *BBC News*, 6 August 2018, https://www.bbc.co.uk/news/uk-politics-45083275 [Accessed November 2021], Lizzie Dearden, 'Islamophobic Incidents Rose 375% after Boris Johnson Compared Muslim Women to "Letterboxes", Figures Show', *The Independent*, 2 September 2019, https://www.independent.co.uk/news/uk/home-news/boris-johnson-muslim-women-letterboxes-burqa-islamphobia-rise-a9088476.html [Accessed November 2021].

11. Dipti Bhatnagar and Syeda Rizwana Hasan, 'Dismantle Patriarchy for System Change', Friends of the Earth International, 31 October 2018, https://www.foei.org/news/system-change-dismantle-patriarchy [Accessed November 2021].

12. Nikesh Shukla, *Brown Baby: A Memoir of Race, Family and Home* (London: Bluebird, 2021).

13. Pink Ladoo Project, www.pinkladoo.org [Accessed March 2021].

Chapter 5

1. Green Park, 'The Colour of Power', *Insights*, https://www.green-park.co.uk/insights/the-colour-of-power/s191468/ [Accessed March 2021].

2. Ijeoma Oluo, *So You Want to Talk About Race* (New York: Seal Press, 2020), 5.

3. Ijeoma Oluo, *So You Want to Talk About Race* (New York: Seal Press, 2020), 5.

4. Resmaa Menakem, *My Grandmother's Hands: Racialized Trauma and the Pathway to Mending Our Hearts and Bodies* (London: Penguin, 2021).

5. Robin DiAngelo, *White Fragility: Why It's so Hard for White People to Talk About Racism* (Boston, MA: Beacon Press, 2018).

6. CIPD, 'Diversity and Inclusion at Work: Facing Up to the Business Case', 2018, https://www.cipd.co.uk/Images/diversity-and-inclusion-at-work_2018-summary_tcm18-44150.pdf [Accessed 1 April 2021].

7. GOV.UK, 'Race in the Workplace', *The McGregor-Smith Review*, 2021.

8. Business in the Community, 'Race', 2021, https://www.bitc.org. uk/race/ [Accessed 15 March 2021].

9. Business in the Community, 'Race', 2021.

10. Equalities and Human Rights Commission, 'Healing a Divided Britain: The Need For a Comprehensive Race Equality Strategy', 2016, https://www.equalityhumanrights.com/sites/default/files/ healing_a_divided_britain_-_the_need_for_a_comprehensive_ race_equality_strategy_final.pdf [Accessed October 2021].

11. Equality and Human Rights Commission, 18 August 2016, 'Healing a Divided Britain: the Need For a Comprehensive Race Equality Strategy', https://www.equalityhumanrights.com/en/publication-download/healing-divided-britain-need-comprehensive-race-equality-strategy [Accessed 30 March 2021].

12. HeForShe, Global Solidarity Movement for Gender Equality, https://www.heforshe.org/en 2019, [Accessed 30 March 2021].

Chapter 6

1. Terry Smith, *Whitelash: Unmasking White Grievance at the Ballot Box* (Cambridge: Cambridge University Press, 2020).

2. Afua Hirsch, *Brit(ish) On Race, Identity and Belonging* (London: Penguin Random House, 2018), 19.

3. Tom Lamont, 'Nish Kumar: "Do They Just Hate My Jokes?"', *The Guardian*, 16 May 2021, https://www.theguardian.com/ culture/2021/may/16/nish-kumar-standup-comedian-do-they-just-hate-my-jokes [Accessed April 2021].

4. Juliet Hooker, 'Black Protest, White Grievance: On the Problem of White Political Imaginations Not Shaped by Loss,' *South Atlantic Quarterly*, 116:3 (2017), 483–504.

5. Juliet Hooker, *Race and the Politics of Solidarity* (Oxford: Oxford University Press, 2009).

6. Kenan Malik: 'Being White Won't Hold Boys Back. Being Working Class Just Might', *The Guardian*, 18 October 2020, https://www. theguardian.com/commentisfree/2020/oct/18/being-white-wont-hold-boys-back-being-working-class-just-might [Accessed April 2021].

7. DfE states that the 'fundamental British values' comprise of democracy, the rule of law, individual liberty, mutual respect for and tolerance of those with different faiths and beliefs, and for those without faith. DfE places a duty on schools, colleges and training providers to prepare pupils for life in modern Britain by

developing their understanding of 'fundamental British values'. British values and citizenship are highlighted in the new Education Inspection Framework 2021.

8. Amy Chua, *Battle Hymn of the Tiger Mother* (New York: Penguin Press, 2011).

9. Reni Eddo-Lodge, 'About Race' (Arts Council England, 2020) at https://www.aboutracepodcast.com/ [Accessed April 2021].

10. Vikram Dodd, 'Black People Nine Times More Likely to Face Stop and Search Than White People', the *Guardian,* 7 October 2020, https://www.theguardian.com/uk-news/2020/oct/27/black-people-nine-times-more-likely-to-face-stop-and-search-than-white-people [Accessed April 2021].

11. Amy Chua, *Political Tribes: Group Instinct and the Fate of Nations* (New York: Penguin, 2018*)*.

12. Some Black women wear weaves as a form of protective styling.

13. Arlie Russell Hochschild, *The Managed Heart: Commercialization of Human Feeling* (Berkeley, CA: The University of California Press, 1983).

Appendix

CONVERSATIONS ON CODE-SWITCHING

I have had many conversations with many individuals over the years about racism and how it manifests in the workplace and, in recent times, about code-switching – what it is and how it plays out in the world of work. I have captured some of the key parts of the more formal discussions that have taken place with friends, acquaintances and those in my professional network below. I am eternally grateful for the openness and honesty, especially because for many people the topic of racial code-switching in particular was not a topic they had previously explored.

White – IT professional

What thoughts cross your mind when you see Black and Asian people in the workplace?
I am drawn to diverse people, and I am usually drawn to Black and to Asian people because of my interest in music and culture and I enjoy learning.

Have you heard of the term code-switching?
No, not before and to me this is shocking. I never knew this happened and I feel saddened by it. I understand that white people do code-switch, but this is different.

What do you think needs to change for progress to be made on race equality?
The entire structure of society needs to change. It is everywhere: for example, in the media, the TV is predominantly white and this doesn't help harness understanding or unity. My own upbringing has been multicultural and I think this is integral to how I view the world and diverse people – it has had a positive impact and I am grateful.

I think there has been change, albeit slow, but it is moving in the right direction and people are more vocal than they ever were. Allies like myself are important for change; I like to educate people and raise awareness.

Black - Medical professional

How do you feel in majority white spaces?
I am comfortable; this has come with age and confidence in who I am and in my capabilities and expertise professionally.

Did you have a level of self-awareness growing up in the context of race?
Yes, I lived in a diverse area of London and from a young age I knew that I was Black, my parents made sure me and my brothers had a strong sense of Black cultural identity.

Does the sketch from Curtis Walker resonate with you? Have you code-switched in a racial context?
Of course; if we didn't, we wouldn't make it in the professional sphere.

Code-switching is something I have done in every job I have had.

What priority does race agenda have in organizations?
Before George Floyd it was quite low – I think most of it is lip service; this is the reason I don't engage with it at work. I know it won't change. I don't think there is an interest or passion or desire to want to create equality. Race equality is seen just like anything else, Health and Safety for example.

After George Floyd – I don't think it is better; I think racial disparities have been highlighted and we can all see how racism actually kills people of colour, we can see this in [the disproportionate numbers of Black and Brown people affected by] Covid-19.

What have organizations done subsequently? – They may be looking at policies, but there is no structural change, nothing has changed on this front.

I think it is a formality – I think it is ticking a box.

Do you think there is a reluctance to call out racism?
Yes – from both white people and people of colour. White people don't want to change the status quo and people of colour don't want to cause a fuss – and to be honest most of us are tired of repeating ourselves!

Do you think white people are aware that people of colour code-switch in a racial context?
No – not at all.

What action needs to be taken for change?
Education. Start from this point and start changing the standard; the standard should not be Eurocentric. It is embedded into everything, from how we see beauty to what we see in the media, in films, to the people leading the organizations we work in – you can't escape it.

Brown – School assistant head

How do you feel when you are in majority white spaces?
Because of my upbringing, I felt quite uncomfortable where I was in Black and Asian spaces. I felt much more comfortable in white spaces. Now, I am more mindful – I am aware of my surroundings and I notice how many people of colour there are. I haven't worked with many teachers of colour. All the heads of schools are white.

Did you have a level of self-awareness growing up in the context of race?
Growing up, I saw myself as no different to my white friends. I grew up in a predominantly white area. We didn't celebrate our culture at home and I didn't learn anything about Sikhism. We didn't celebrate or mark any religious or cultural days. I felt white. Maybe my parents thought this was best for us. Thinking about it, I think they code-switched because they felt that this might be better for us children. They wanted us to do well.

My husband is white; I didn't feel I would have a connection with an Indian person, [or] be able to cope with it due to my upbringing, maybe.

Does the sketch from Curtis Walker resonate with you – have you heard of code-switching?
No, because as I said – I didn't feel any different to the white norm. I didn't feel Asian.

Do you think that white people are aware that we have this internal dialogue that takes place in our minds?
No, and I have not thought about it so consciously; however, now thinking about it and talking to you – I can see it.

What do you feel needs to happen and what needs to change to make progress?
Education is key. If all children see around them is one type of person being held up as the norm, this is a problem. We need different role models everywhere and especially in the school setting. Diversity currently is on the periphery; however, it needs to be weaved in as the norm – not something to be celebrated once a month for example. The narrative surrounding British Values that is to be promoted in schools is problematic also, I can see how this 'othering' from a young age sows the seeds for prejudice and bias later on in life.

Brown – Pharmacist

How do you feel when you are in majority white spaces?
I always know where I am and what my surroundings are. My profession is however quite diverse and I enjoy that about it.

Did you have a level of self-awareness growing up in the context of race?
Yes, I went to a mixed school but I didn't really give it too much thought because my school was quite mixed.

Does the sketch from Curtis Walker resonate with you – have you heard of code-switching?
I haven't heard of it before but I can most certainly resonate with it. I think I have code-switched because you want to appear professional – that said, most senior consultants I work with are from a diverse background so I think it's more about appearing professional. Although – thinking about it, I anglicize my name so it is easier for white people. I am aware that if I want to progress at an executive level, I need to code-switch. I see that other Black and Asian people do this that are senior. It's almost a prerequisite.

Do you think that white people are aware that we have this internal dialogue that takes place in our minds?
No. I don't think so.

What do you feel needs to happen and what needs to change to make progress?
I hope that as more diverse people get into senior positions there is less of a need to. But we are not talking about this anywhere. I think it is good to get this out. The standard of whiteness is the norm, but we live in a diverse society and therefore all bring our uniqueness (if it was to be accepted) to the table, which can be a wonderful thing.

Black - Lawyer

How do you feel when you are in majority white spaces?
I do always feel on edge, I am never myself – although it does depend on context.

Generally, I am a confident person and in public I can be myself; I am less concerned. However, I completely change when I step into the office.

I change my diction, how I stand and my body language. I am very aware of how I will be viewed because of my skin colour. I do not want to be seen as being aggressive. If I am annoyed or frustrated in the office, I feel I can't show my anger or frustration – it would negatively impact on me. I feel like I can't respond in a natural way.

I am conscious that I will be taken in the wrong way and I also feel that if I put a foot wrong – I could quite easily be made redundant.

Did you have a level of self-awareness growing up in a racial context?

Yes, very much so. My parents made a conscious effort to raise us to be aware. It wasn't abnormal for us to watch the civil rights era on television so we were prepared and realistic about the struggle ahead. I attended both a diverse and not-so-diverse school – when you are in the minority the difference is a prominent feature and this is perfect for derogatory remarks and racial tensions. And if that wasn't enough, I was encouraged to get into sports too!

Does the sketch from Curtis Walker resonate with you – have you heard of code-switching?
Yes, the sketch massively resonates with me! You conform cos you are in the minority – you can't be yourself. The way I code-switch is to appear as less threatening (in their eyes). To be very conscious and mindful of your demeanour and I try to 'small' myself.

What impact has this had, if any?
There is a real distrust of white people. I don't feel I am able to be myself or let my guard down. It takes me a lot of time for me to trust. I am speaking from past experiences, and you use your experiences to navigate your way forward. It is difficult to be open and express how you really feel cos you're not the majority.

Do you think that white people are aware that we have this internal dialogue that takes place in our minds?
Not a clue! I think they are completely oblivious! White people want to see you as a Black version of themselves, not all the intricacies that come with being Black.

What do you feel needs to happen and what needs to change to make progress?
People need to open their eyes to the reality of the world and

society that we are living in: how society is set up in the context of race. Only when you understand the infrastructure and the setup of society and who benefits from the infrastructure can you start to address the real problems and issues.

It's really important to understand historical context. The impact of colonialism on Black and Asian people's exploitation has been the foundation of racism and it seems to me that white people are happy with this situation; the status quo benefits them.

I feel in most contexts Black people are stigmatized and we can see in the most recent example of the Black Lives Matter protests Black people being referred to as thugs.

The question that white people have to ask themselves is, what have they done recently to be anti-racist?

I feel it's really important that Black people understand their own history and are masters of their own destiny in order to understand the current environment. It's really important you know the past; if you're ignorant to the past then you in a vulnerable position.

I am a pessimist. I don't think there is any hope. And yes, that's sad, but that is the real fact of it.

Black - Professional

How do you feel when you are in majority white spaces?
Hyper-aware that I am in that space. You need to moderate yourself because I think we are always being judged, I went to quite a mixed school, however, college was predominantly white and I felt intimidated, but you learn how to adjust yourself to be in that space. I learned how to be by observing others.

Did you have a level of self-awareness growing up in a racial context?

I always knew I was Black, I came from Jamaican parentage and this was very much embedded in my upbringing.

Does the sketch from Curtis Walker resonate with you – have you heard of code-switching?
I am very aware that I can be misunderstood as being aggressive but I am always myself – perhaps that is why I have been overlooked for promotion.

What impact has this had, if any?
A huge impact – it takes a lot of energy; we have to think, employ certain skills. You are always conscious of how you are perceived as a Black person or a person of colour. I find that we have to go the extra mile, be better than the average person.

Do you think that white people are aware that we have this internal dialogue that takes place in our minds?
NO!

What do you feel needs to happen and what needs to change to make progress?
Education and raising awareness of history. I find it to be sad that young people have ensured this.

Brown – Senior accountant

How do you feel when you are in majority white spaces?
I feel different. I don't feel a pressure to conform to whiteness, but I see that not confirming creates a blockage because your talent and ability will only get you so far. Not conforming to the standards of whiteness can be a hindrance to success at the senior levels. You do not fit in. I feel to progress you have to be exceptionally better than your white counterparts.

Did you have a level of self-awareness growing up in a racial context?
Yes, I was born in Scotland and it was very white at a time when we were the only Asian family on the road. In addition, English was not my first language and I was very aware of the cultural differences. My family kept themselves to themselves. We didn't interact so much with others outside family.

Does the sketch from Curtis Walker resonate with you – have you heard of code-switching?
No, but I know that a lot of people do it. As a Muslim, I find that alcohol plays a part in the professional culture and when you don't conform to this – it impacts on your career.

What impact has this had, if any?
I think the cultural nuances that exist in different communities are not accepted because they are deemed to be different. Most organizations have diversity policies to encourage diversity; however, in practice it is very different. There is a huge lack of understanding. I find it draining, and because of my faith I'm judged regardless.

Do you think that white people are aware that we have this internal dialogue that takes place in our minds?
Yes, I do. I think most senior managers that are very senior are intelligent; however, they choose to ignore what they don't want to see or address.

What do you feel needs to happen and what needs to change to make progress?
Effort in actually making a change. It can't be ignored or it will continue; people need to be treated as human beings and we need to remove the layers that society has placed on us. I think an open and a positive attitude to learning is important.

Brown - Higher education professional

How do you feel when you are in majority white spaces?
Uncomfortable; I deflect with humour. I work in a white environment. I feel I have to be white to succeed in my role. I can really see how privilege plays a role in success. As I climb the career ladder, I see how significant the disparity is.

Did you have a level of self-awareness growing up in a racial context?
Yes – I grew up being certain of my identity and who I was, however, just the impact of Brownness didn't come into fruition until a lot later – in adulthood.

Does the sketch from Curtis Walker resonate with you – have you heard of code-switching?
Yes, very much so! I consciously switch to the point that I deny my existence. I am always thinking about the audience. I don't want to be pigeonholed in a certain type of way or be stereotyped – and this is always in a racialized context.

What impact has this had, if any?
It has had a massive impact in my career – I don't want their [white people's] biases to impact on me. Everyone code-switches, but ethnicity is different.

Do you think that white people are aware that we have this internal dialogue that takes place in our minds?
No I don't think it crosses their minds. They haven't got a clue!

What do you feel needs to happen and what needs to change to make progress?
White people to take accountability and to have open conversations with a degree of honesty.

White – IT professional

What thoughts cross your mind when you see Black and Asian people in the workplace?
I think context is important – in the work environment its very non-threatening. However, in the media it is portrayed differently. If I am honest, the first thought that comes to my mind is that they are in the organization to fill some sort of quota.

[I ask if his organization has quotas – to which he replies no]

It's only after I get to know them and I feel they are competent that my initial thoughts fade.

Have you heard of the term code-switching?
No. [I explain the term.] *Oh yeah, white people do this too. It is a mental process to fit in and be included. All people assimilate. What if you had a very visual birthmark? The issue that you're referring to is as a result of the slave trade. However, code-switching is about mentally preparing yourself. You can think of it as similar to a job interview – you need to prepare to impress and fit in. Everyone does it. I don't think it is different really.*

What do you think needs to change for progress to be made on race equality?
We are not there yet. There is a lot of reflection that needs to come about. But it's important to remember that people always smell out weaknesses – accents etc.; these are used as weapons to villainize.

Black people and people of colour should be themselves – believe in themselves. I also feel we need to stop talking in terms of ethnicity and race. We should stop referring to people as Black person or Asian person.

Black - Finance professional

How do you feel when you in you're in majority-white places?
I am very nervous about the impression I might give. Especially as I have a Caribbean accent. I am scared, as I feel I will be judged cos I am not one of them. I don't have the space to make an error. I feel if I make an error, all Black people are making an error.

I am very nervous; I try not to come across too ambitious or eager – I feel like I have to small myself – but not too small so that it may affect career progression opportunities. I try to be accommodating and not too threatening. When I am in a majority-white space, I try to identity commonality very quickly.

Trust is very important and I have to observe for a period of time before I can let my guard down a little.

When did you notice you were Black? Did you have a level of self-awareness growing up in a racial context?
I noticed I was Black when I came to the UK! I am from the Virgin Islands and, of course, it was never a thing. Back home I could see myself represented in all roles and at all levels – here is it so different. There was a moment when I was shouted down by the bus driver, on the bus, when I handed them a note – I had not realized that back then you needed the correct change. I felt everyone stare and I was really embarrassed. In this moment I felt Black – it is hard to explain, but I felt that I was talked to in that manner due to the colour of my skin.

When I first arrived in the UK I didn't understand the nuances and why my Black friends felt disengaged; however, I get it now. Back home you are allowed to be who you are because you are accepted; it is most certainly not the case here in the UK!

At home I was taught history from the Black perspective but it wasn't ever anything that was negatively perceived or had any negative conations to me until I arrived in the UK to study.

Does the sketch from Curtis Walker resonate with you – have you heard of code-switching?
Yes! 100 per cent. I can really relate to this. I do not show exactly who I am to the extent that I tone down my accent – it will be too much for them; so I change myself so white people can accept me.

What impact, if any, does this have?
It is so natural to me that it has become second nature. I ask colleagues and friends to read over my emails to ensure the tone is right, that it doesn't come across [as] aggressive. I would hate to be called that – there are so many connotations attached to it. There is a psychological impact that comes with code-switching.

Do you think white people are aware of the internal dialogue that takes place in our minds?
Maybe – it depends on the organization and the culture that exists. On the whole however, probably not!

What can be done to make progress in this area?
Honesty! And acceptance that it will get uncomfortable! White people are indirectly benefiting from slavery and the complicity is dangerous. Silence is an agreement and if you are watching from the sidelines, then you're a part of the problem! The real history needs to be uncovered from Black historians.

White – Higher education professional

What thoughts cross your mind when you see Black and Asian people in the workplace?
A relief! I came from Wales and moved to Birmingham as I wanted to live somewhere that was diverse. However, coming from a very white Wales, I felt very ignorant and very conscious. I moved to Birmingham in the early 2000s and racial tensions and Islamophobia was emerging strong and fast. I didn't want to offend or say the wrong things.

I genuinely enjoy being a part of a diverse community.

Have you heard of the term code-switching?
No I haven't. **[I explain]** *– I can see what you mean. That sounds very exhausting! To some extent, everyone code-switches – you try to fit into the majority culture. I can draw parallels with social mobility and class background. These issues intersect with one another.*

What do you think needs to change for progress to be made on race equality?
If people don't understand the points you have raised, such as code-switching, then it can't be addressed. This is not an issue that needs to be addressed by Black and Asian people. This is a white people's issue. Once code-switching and other aspects of racism are explained and out there in the public it can create a greater understanding. It seems that code-switching is esoteric – however I assume most Black and Asian people experience this on some level.

White – Senior media engineer

What thoughts cross your mind when you see Black and Asian people in the workplace?
No feelings evoked. I think I am neutral. I always think to myself I hope they don't feel uncomfortable being a minority.

What do you think about code-switching – do you know it happens?
I have never thought about it in terms of ethnicity, although I have seen white people code-switch – everyone does to some extent. But now you have explained it I see it very differently – thank you for this insight.

What do you think needs to change for progress to be made on race equality?
There has been some change; however, of course the UK is not there yet. Working in media I can see a major shift in terms of who is represented, but it is way too slow and the decision-makers are mainly white. More people should make a point of the lack of representation [in senior positions]; then code-switching might not take place.

Black – Senior solicitor

How do you feel when you're in majority white places?
As a solicitor you notice the differences. I did wonder if I was appointed to fit a quota. There was only ever one or two of us and I felt that there would never be any more 'cos they had ticked the diversity box.

I feel in some ways, because my ways were very 'white' it was easier for me to navigate the majority-white culture, I wanted to conform and to be successful – when I look back, I feel sad.

I conformed massively, but mainly in terms of gender, race wasn't an issue for me because, as I said, I grew up believing that I had the right to be anywhere I wanted to be. That said, I understand that I believed that, but that is not how the world viewed me. I acted manly because I wanted to fit in – I was different, but I didn't want them to notice that difference. Some Black people may have described me as a coconut.

Did you have a level of self-awareness in terms of identity growing up in a racial context?
I am Nigerian and at the age of one I was brought up by white foster parents in Norfolk. It was very white, but that wasn't a problem. I knew I was different but my parents bought me up to feel that I belonged and I had a right to be anywhere. In fact, I felt like an outsider [both] when I visited Nigeria and at home with my foster parents. I started to feel different when I was older. I realized I liked being in an environment that was predominately Black and in the summer there was a weekend in Great Yarmouth that would bring crowds of mainly Black people for a soul weekend. I loved this and felt it was really nice to be amongst people who looked like me.

At University is where I became more aware of my cultural background. It was accepted that the Black kids hang around with the Black kids.

Does the sketch from Curtis Walker resonate with you – have you heard of code-switching?
Yes, definitely. In fact, I have turned the radio station to Classic FM when I know that we are off to a hearing of whatever. We are all conforming, in so many ways.

Now, with age, confidence and the fact that I am a senior partner in a firm, I want to bring my authentic self to work. Although progress is slow – we are in a very different place to where we were some twenty years ago.

179

What impact, if any does this have?
On me, I am not too sure. I try not to think about it too much. I try to push through. I have a good support system at home – I lick my wounds at home. I am very optimistic – if I was to stop and look into it too deeply I wouldn't go out.

I have felt like I am not worthy when I have been in majority-white spaces.

Do you think white people are aware of the internal dialogue that takes place in our minds?
They haven't got a clue, and how could they? It is privilege. They can never have this understanding.

What can be done to make progress in this area?
Black Lives Matter has provided a space – Black people, more than Asian people, are disadvantaged. I think Black people should be vocal, especially if you are senior. We must keep talking about this. My worry is that the focus will move to the next big thing.

White – Senior manager

What do you feel when you see Black and Asian people in the workplace?
Happy! Diversity is a positive attribute to any organization and I enjoy the diverse mix-up of people. Diversity makes me feel comfortable – I think that's because my background is mixed heritage, although I appreciate I don't look it and I can quite easily pass as white. I think people make assumptions about my ethnicity and I never really talk about it.

What do you think about code-switching?
I understand that people try to assimilate and I would consider

myself to have some level of awareness. I find it fascinating and I have a real interest in cognitive bias.

What do you think needs to change to move forward on race equality?
Educate younger generations. There must be open and honest conversations about race in Western society. It is for those in the majority – that is, white people – to make changes. It's important to find common ground, to build relationships and entrust and to be aware of who you're working with, what their backgrounds are, what their journeys are. It's for us to raise our own awareness.

Brown – Ex-academy professional cricketer/ marketing professional

How do you feel in majority white spaces?
I feel pretty comfortable, but I am aware that I am in a white space.

Did you have a level of self-awareness in terms of identity growing up in a racial context?
Yes, but most of my friends are white; I played football and there were not many Asian players, so in school and out of school my circle was white.

Have you code-switched?
I wouldn't speak of it as code-switching; it is more of a process, it is second nature. I changed most when I went to college; it was very affluent, white and middle class and I changed my behaviour, but I think more to fit in generally. I am not sure if I would say it was code-switching; I don't think so.

What impact does code-switching have?
You are always aware that you are a person of colour and I think the expectations are different. I noticed when I started to play cricket that this was the case – especially when compared to white cricket players and being reprimanded for the same behaviours they displayed.

It has a negative impact and it reduced diversity of thought and individuality. In some cases, you are not accepted for who you are.

What do you think needs to change to move forward on race equality?
Exposure to different people.

Brown – Finance professional/ semi-professional cricketer

How do you feel in majority white spaces?
You're always hyper-alert and aware that you are in a white space.

Did you have a level of self-awareness in terms of identity growing up in a racial context?
Yes, when I came to the UK perhaps – I had a very strong family structure, and grew up with a strong sense of identity and faith. I wasn't born here, but my strong family make-up made it easier to adapt to this culture.

Have you code-switched?
Of course, you have to code-switch. There is knowing your audience and good communication and then there is code-switching. Code-switching, I agree, is trying to fit into white-ness. I am able to say I code-switch more openly now as I

have become much more confident and senior in my profession. You are not able to climb up the career ladder without code-switching.

Turning to sport, in particular cricket, most people of colour will code-switch at some point. I know many Muslim players, for example, that drink alcohol and later regret it. Why do they do it? To code-switch, to fit in. Bias plays its role, and affinity bias can have a positive impact in a player's cricketing career.

Racism exists and it is very real. I am not referring to the overt sort of racism – I am talking about structural racism. Don't get me wrong, overt racism is rife in sport but to some extent you can brush that off (although it takes its toll). It is because of institutional racism that I feel I didn't make it professionally. There wasn't anything that anyone said or did – but I just didn't make it. Why? I'm not sure, but I know my stats were excellent – good enough to be playing at a professional level.

From a young age my parents have drummed into me that I have to be better, better than white people to actually make it; and not just marginally better, exceptionally better.

What impact does code-switching have?

It is not necessarily a bad thing – it comes with some positives; it has allowed me to become successful. I do code-switch and will always code-switch, I think. I don't think we are there yet as a country to not code-switch. I think you are right; the standard of whiteness is what we all ultimately aim towards, and it is far too powerful. People of colour have two options. They can accept that this is the system in which we live and be very happy because they live in their bubble – or you can address and challenge. What Black Lives Matter has allowed us to do is provide a space to challenge – however, even that can come with repercussions.

What do you think needs to change to move forward on race equality?
To be successful you really need the guidance and support. Code-switching can only take you so far. I think, for people of colour, you really need a network of people that you can call upon for guidance. These don't have to be other people of colour; it is people who know how the system works and who have experience who can guide you. The number of times I have sought advice from people I have looked up to for a variety of reasons. It is good to have this. I have actively sought out mentors who I admire and my advice to Black and Brown people is always to do the same. Approach people and ask for advice, opinions and views.

In terms of institutional racism and the system; well, that's too big to address!

Brown - Teacher

How do you feel in majority white spaces?
I feel fine, but I went for an interview and everyone was white and I thought 'I'm not going to get this job.' I subsequently did, but that I was quite was aware of my ethnicity – more so because it was so white.

Did you have a level of self-awareness in terms of identity growing up in a racial context?
Yes, I was aware that I was Indian. My friends were predominantly white so I knew I was different in terms of how I was brought up.

Does the sketch from Curtis Walker resonate with you – have you heard of code-switching?
Yes, but I think I just adapt; however, maybe code-switching is so subconscious I don't even realize it.

What impact has this had, if any?

I need to process what we have discussed because there must be an impact but I have never thought about it. What am I adapting to? This is what I need to reflect on further because for me it is just normal – but you are right, the 'normal' is what is everywhere and it might be that I adapt to become 'normal'.

Do you think that white people are aware that we have this internal dialogue that takes place in our minds?

It is never spoken about in this context; so I doubt it.

What do you feel needs to happen and what needs to change to make progress?

I feel my role in education is pivotal to making a change. I can redefine 'normal' in the way I teach, the books I use at school, the people we talk about, the days we mark and celebrate, the art we study; in fact, there might be quite a few ways. However, that is not enough, is it? It needs a national approach not an individual one. If there was a collective agreement that this is what we want to do in a country that would be a wonderful thing.

Brown - Social care professional

How do you feel in majority white spaces?

I often struggle when I am new in a work environment. I feel nervous about sharing who I am fully. I feel that white people don't always understand people of colour. I am conscious that I will be taken in the wrong way and I rarely speak about racism or identity politics and I naturally gravitate to people of colour in the workplace – I think it is a comfort thing. But I am also mindful about how this might be perceived and whether this may impact [me] negatively.

Did you have a level of self-awareness in terms of identity growing up in a racial context?
[I did, in] secondary school. It was predominantly white and I experienced racism. I also noticed the cultural differences and when I was growing up school was a very white experience in terms of what we learned about, read, [for example,] the historical figures.

Does the sketch from Curtis Walker resonate with you – have you heard of code-switching?
Massively; in fact, I have done this very thing. I haven't heard of code-switching, however, having now heard of it I would say I do code-switch to fit in, but I don't do this consciously. I do it because I don't want to be judged negatively.

What impact has this had, if any?
I haven't thought about it, so I am not too sure – I think there is probably a lot of subconscious stuff that goes on.

Do you think that white people are aware that we have this internal dialogue that takes place in our minds?
No – not at all – why would they [be]?

What do you feel needs to happen and what needs to change to make progress?
Before now, I never thought to address it. I didn't have the language, [but] having had this discussion things seem to click into place. Organizations need to address this. It is really difficult for Black and Brown people to talk about this. Even now, as I am speaking to you memories of little incidents come back to me, and it angers me.

Acknowledgements

The authors would like to thank Jonathan Reuvid – without his support and encouragement, this book would not exist. They would also like to thank their families and close friends for bearing with them, helping with ideas and providing the space to write this.

Vanisha Parmar would also like to thank the people she spoke to whilst exploring racial code-switching, in particular, the following people for their honesty, openness, support and vulnerability:
Usmaan Awan, Kiran Bennet, Paul Bouchier, Jeannie Brooks, Neil Budhia, Kumaldeep Chagger, Yetunde Dania, Lloyd Davis, A Gaskin, Colin G., Anila Godhania, Shanawaz Jamil, Preeya Mistry, Dr Tina Mistry, Rita Narendra, Anisha Parmar, Minesh Parmar, Vanda Parmar, Kate Parsons, Priya N. Patel, Brinder Phagura, Sarine Pickering, Helena Poggi, Malcolm Taylor, Basiru Terry, Michael Williams and Monique Worgs.

About the Authors

Vanisha Parmar is a passionate and committed change agent and an anti-racism advocate. She is a diversity specialist with twenty years' experience of working in large, complex organizations including the education sector and legal sector, nonprofits and the third sector. She is a law graduate, but decided not to pursue a career as a solicitor and instead studied a Masters in Race and Ethnic Studies at the University of Warwick. She was recently named in the Women in Law's UK's top 100 future power list for her work in the legal profession and regularly speaks on diversity, bias and anti-racism in addition to other areas of equality. Her work includes supporting organizations in creating strategic change, as well as providing solutions at an operational level.

Aseia Rafique has long championed equality, equity, diversity and inclusion – in particular, in the area of women's rights. She has extensive experience of working across many sectors to challenge sexism, racism, stereotypes and misogyny against women. Running her own business has meant Aseia has been able to support, advocate and promote inclusivity across diverse business organizations in the third sector, education and law. Working in equality, diversity and inclusion has meant realizing the potential to drive change, to help others overcome adversity and to advocate the rights of others. She studied for a Masters in Gender and International Development at the University of Warwick and has lived and worked abroad in Harbin, China.